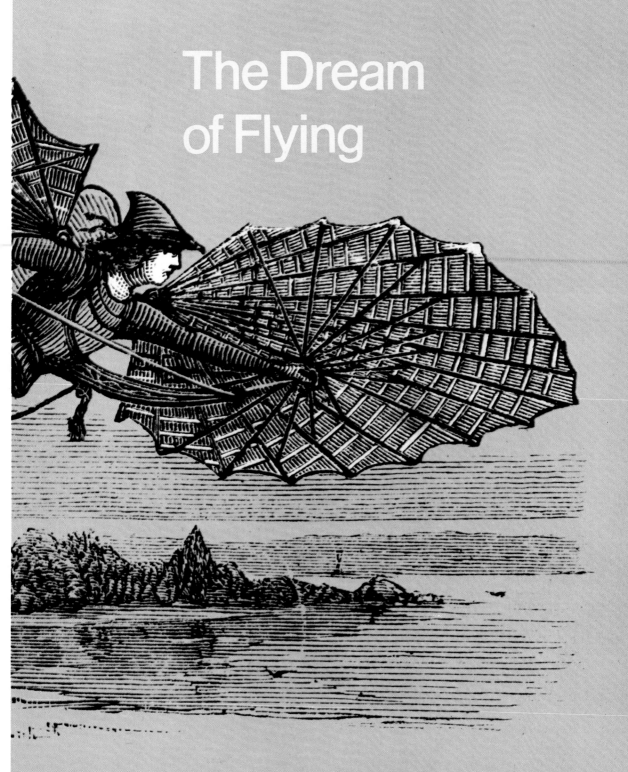

The Dream of Flying

Ancient flying stories

Old, old stories tell of people who found ways to fly—ways that, of course, could never really have worked.

An ancient Chinese story, more than 3,700 years old, tells of Prince Ki-Kung-Shi, who built a flying chariot that was powered by the wind. The prince flew great distances in it, high above the clouds. But the Emperor Cheng Tang ordered the chariot to be destroyed. He feared that too many people might learn the secret of flying, and the sky would soon be full of flying chariots.

A three-thousand-year-old Greek myth tells of another man who supposedly invented a way to fly. He was Daedalus, a skilled craftsman and inventor who worked for King Minos, ruler of the island of Crete.

Daedalus offended Minos, and Minos had him and his son, Icarus, thrown into prison. Daedalus and Icarus managed to escape, but they were trapped on the island, and the soldiers of Minos were hunting for them. So Daedalus made two pairs of big wings, using feathers, thread, and wax. Daedalus and Icarus fastened these wings to their arms. Then, flapping their arms, they flew away from the island and headed across the sea toward Italy.

But young Icarus was so thrilled by being able to fly that he grew careless. Joyfully, he soared higher and higher, getting closer and closer to the sun. Finally, the wax that held the wing feathers in place melted in the sun's heat. Icarus plunged to his death in the sea, far, far below.

Stories such as these tell us that even long, long ago, people wanted to fly even though they were a little afraid of the idea.

The winged men

All through history there were men who tried to fly as birds do. They made wings out of wood, cloth, leather, and feathers. They went to high places, fastened the wings to their arms, and jumped off. They believed that they could fly if they flapped their wings.

More than nine hundred years ago a monk known as Oliver of Malmesbury attached a wing to each arm and jumped off the roof of a church in England. He flapped his arms as fast as he could—but he fell straight to the ground and broke both his legs.

About five hundred years ago a man named Senecio put on a pair of wings he had made and jumped off a tower in Nuremberg, Germany. He merely broke an arm.

Some 450 years ago, a man named Bolori jumped off the high steeple of the Cathedral of Troyes, in France. Of course, this poor man's wings failed him, and he was killed.

About three hundred years ago, a Frenchman named Besnier fashioned four big leather squares on poles. Holding the poles across his shoulders, he jumped off the roof of his house, pumping the poles up and down. Naturally, he failed to fly, but he managed to land without getting hurt.

A little more than 240 years ago, a French nobleman, the Marquis de Bacqueville, announced that he was going to fly across the Seine River. A great many people came to watch him try. He attached big wings to his arms and legs, then jumped off the roof of a house beside the river. But he came down on the deck of a boat that was sailing down the river and broke both his legs.

Today, we smile at the foolhardy attempts of those men, and feel sorry for those who were killed or hurt. But they were really heroes. They believed so strongly that people should fly that they were willing to risk their lives to learn how to do it.

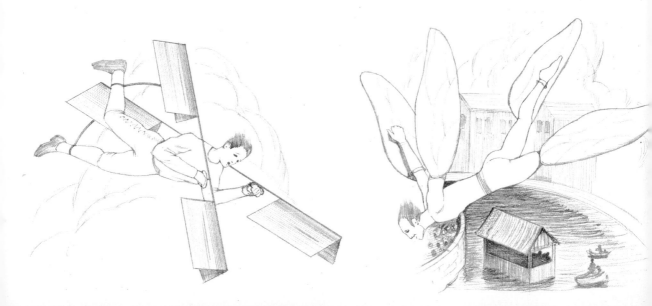

The artist who dreamed of flying

One of the greatest artists who ever lived also designed a parachute and drew plans for a flying machine that could carry a person. The artist was Leonardo da Vinci, who lived in Italy some five hundred years ago. He painted two of the most famous of all pictures, the *Mona Lisa* and *The Last Supper*.

But Leonardo was also something of a scientist as well as a marvelous artist. He firmly believed that it would be possible to build a machine with which a person could fly. He made many drawings and plans for such machines, and also built models of them.

Leonardo thought a flying machine would have to have

Leonardo's drawing for the body of an ornithopter, a flying machine designed to fly by flapping the wings.

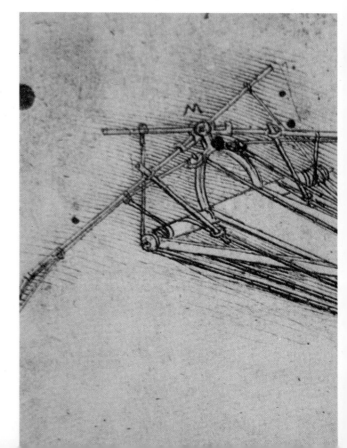

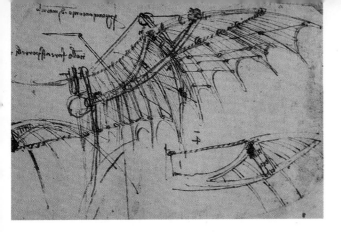

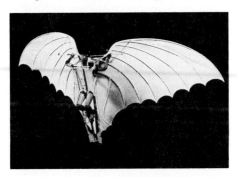

A drawing by Leonardo (above) of the wings for his ornithopter, and a model ornithopter (below) built using Leonardo's drawings.

wings that flapped, like the wings of a bird or bat. His sketches show many clever ideas for machinery to make wings flap. However, Leonardo's flying machines would not have worked even if they had been built.

But one of Leonardo's ideas would have worked. One of his drawings, done in 1495, shows a man floating down beneath what looks like a big cloth pyramid—a kind of parachute. So Leonardo da Vinci invented the parachute about five hundred years ago. But nearly three hundred years went by before anyone actually tried out the great artist's invention.

Leonardo's drawing for a parachute

Flying machine ideas

While some men were trying to fly by fastening wings to their arms, others were trying to build machines that could carry people into the sky. A little more than three hundred years ago Father Francesco de Lana, an Italian priest, worked out an idea for what he called an "aerial ship." The priest's idea was to fasten four large hollow balls made of very thin copper to a small boat and pump all the air out of the copper balls. Father de Lana thought this would make the balls lighter than air and so they would float into the sky, carrying the boat with them.

Father de Lana was right in thinking that taking all the air out of the balls would make them lighter than air. But if Father de Lana had been able to remove all the air inside the balls, the pressure of the air surrounding them would have squashed them flat. So, his idea would not have worked. If Father de Lana could have filled the copper balls with a lighter-than-air gas like that put into balloons now, they probably would have lifted the boat into the air. However, at that time no one knew there was such a thing as a gas that was lighter than air.

At any rate, Father de Lana gets credit for having the first good idea for what is called a lighter-than-air aircraft. His "aerial ship"

An artist's picture of
Father Francesco da Lana's
idea for a flying machine.

was actually the great-great-grandfather of
such airships as the Goodyear blimp of today.

About forty years after Father de Lana
thought up his machine, another priest
invented a different sort of flying machine.
Father Laurenço de Gusmão, a Brazilian who
lived in Portugal, built a craft with a bird's
head carved on the front and big wings on
the sides. The wings flapped when a person
sitting in the craft pulled a handle back and
forth. A big sail was stretched over the boat,
like a parachute. But of course Father de
Gusmão's machine never got off the ground.

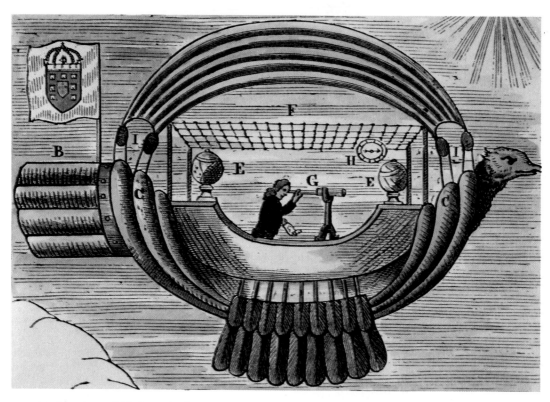

an old drawing of Father de Gusmão's flying machine

Karl Meerwein's 1781 flying machine

About fifty-five years later, in 1764, Melchior Bauer, a German, drew up plans for a flying machine. It was a box on four wheels, with a big wing fastened to it. The pilot was supposed to stand in the box and row the machine into the air using a big double paddle.

In 1781, another German, Karl Meerwein, built a machine that almost worked. It was a huge wing, shaped like a flat American football. Meerwein lay stretched out under the wing, in the middle, and was able to glide just above the ground for a very short distance.

None of these flying machines had a good way of getting up into the air and staying there. But a way to do that was about to be discovered.

Up We Go!

The first real "flying machine"

It was a warm June day in 1783, and there was great excitement in the little French town of Vidalon les Annonay. Two brothers, Étienne and Joseph Montgolfier, who ran the town's paper factory, had promised that something wonderful was going to happen on that day. They had made a huge bag out of cloth and paper, and they claimed they were going to make this bag fly.

Of course, most people didn't believe them. After all, only creatures that had wings to flap, such as birds, bugs, and bats, could fly. There was no way a human being could make something fly. But it would be fun to watch the silly brothers play with their giant bag, and fun to laugh at them when it didn't work.

The bag was stretched over a wooden frame, with its open end facing the ground. Under this open part, the Montgolfier brothers had built a smoky fire out of damp straw and bunches of sheep's wool. There were a number of ropes fastened to the edge of the bag, and men were holding onto them.

The crowd buzzed and chattered and giggled and laughed. But gradually, people began to grow quiet because they saw that the big bag had started to swell up. Fatter and fatter it grew, until it became a huge globe with a tapering bottom. Everyone could see that it was beginning to rise into the air.

In fact, as the bag grew larger, the men holding the ropes had to strain with all their

might to hold it down. Other men rushed to
help them. Soon there were eight men
hanging onto the ropes while the swollen bag
jiggled and jumped, trying to float away.

Then, one of the Montgolfier brothers
shouted "Let go." The men holding the ropes
obeyed. The bag shot straight up into the
sky, seeming to get smaller and smaller as it
rose higher and higher. The crowd yelled and

applauded. The Montgolfiers had indeed made their giant bag fly.

Actually, the brothers had been secretly experimenting for a long time. One of them had discovered that paper envelopes, made at their factory, seemed to grow light in weight and lift up into the air when held above a fire. The brothers began to make special little paper bags that would sail up into the air when held over a fire. So the brothers knew their big bag would work. But they did not really know why. They thought the smoke from the fire of wool and straw made the paper bags rise.

Of course, it was really the hot air that made the bags rise. When air gets hot, it rises. Hot air from the fires the brothers built would rise up into the bags until they were full of enough hot air to lift them up into the sky. When the air inside the bags started to cool, the bags would slowly drift back to earth.

That day, June 4, 1783, was really an important day in history. The Montgolfiers' big bag rose some six thousand feet (1,800 meters) into the sky. It looked so much like a big ball that people called it a *ballon* (balloon), which means something like "big ball" in French. The Montgolfiers' balloon was the first known "flying machine." On the day it rose into the air, the conquest of the sky began.

The "test pilots"

Soon after the successful flight of their balloon, the Montgolfier brothers made another startling announcement. They planned to make a balloon that could carry a man into the sky.

However, the king of France sent word that he would not allow this. Along with many others, he feared it might be dangerous for a person to fly into the sky in a balloon. No one knew what might happen to someone who went high up into the air. He might become ill or even die.

The Montgolfiers decided they had better find out if balloon flying would be safe. They thought that if they sent some animals up and the animals returned safely, people could safely go up in balloons, too. So, they asked the king's permission to send up some animals in one of their balloons.

The king agreed to this, and on September 19, 1783, the brothers sent up a balloon from the courtyard of the king's palace. A large basket fastened to the bottom of the balloon carried a duck, a rooster, and a sheep.

The king, queen, and all the courtiers watched with wonder as the balloon rose higher and higher. Astronomers watched through telescopes, and estimated that the balloon reached an altitude of about 1,640 feet (500 meters).

In a few minutes, the balloon began to descend toward a nearby woods. Messengers were sent to see if the three animals had survived. They found that the basket had broken open when the balloon landed. But all three animals had escaped and were safe and sound.

So the first living creatures to leave the earth in a flying machine were a duck, a rooster, and a sheep. The flight proved that it would be safe for people to go up in a balloon.

The first people to fly

Now that living creatures had gone into the sky and survived, everyone wondered who would be the first person to make such a flight. Jean François Pilâtre de Rozier, a young French scientist, went to the king and volunteered. The king gave his permission.

At once, the Montgolfier brothers began to make a special balloon that could carry a man. It was the biggest balloon they had yet made—fifty feet (15 meters) wide and more than seventy-five feet (23 m) high. Around the bottom, or "neck," of the balloon they made a platform on which a man could stand. Inside the neck hung an iron pot in which a fire would be kept burning to send hot air up into the balloon and keep it flying. The man on the platform could feed the fire by reaching in through a hole in the neck of the balloon.

In order to assure complete safety, Pilâtre de Rozier took three practice tests in the balloon. For these tests, long ropes held the balloon so it could not float free. Everything seemed to be all right, so the flight was set for the morning of November 21, 1783. The balloon was taken to a little park in a woods outside Paris.

Pilâtre de Rozier had decided not to make this historic flight alone. A friend, François d'Arlandes, a captain in the French army, would go with him.

On the morning of the flight, a large crowd gathered to watch the wonderful event. Pilâtre de Rozier and Captain d'Arlandes stepped onto the balloon platform and waited. As the big balloon slowly filled with hot air, it began to swell up.

Then disaster struck. A violent gust of wind caught the half-filled balloon and sent it skidding across the ground. Pilâtre de Rozier and the captain were not hurt, but the balloon was ripped.

The Montgolfier brothers did not give up, however. While men dragged the

balloon back to the starting place, the two
brothers rushed to find some women who
could sew up the rips.

However, this took so long a time that the
crowd grew restless. Most of the people
began to think the flight would never take
place. Some shouted that it was all a fake.

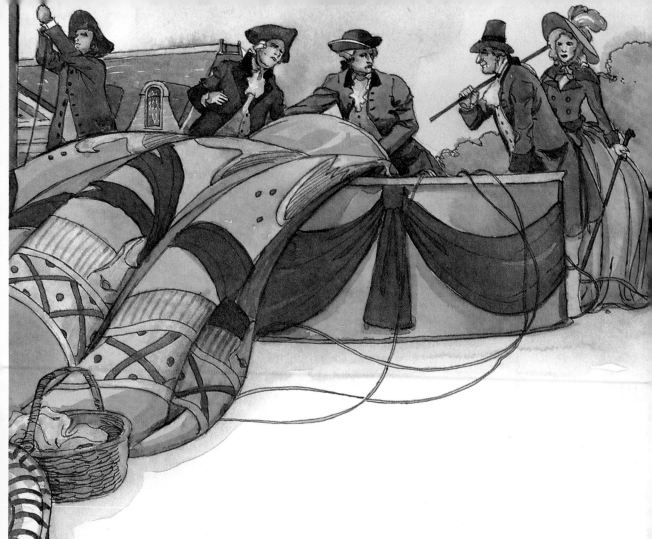

One man came up to the balloon and leaned
over the edge of the platform. "I don't
suppose you will take off?" he asked Pilâtre
de Rozier.

"Indeed I will," the young scientist
answered.

Once again the balloon slowly filled up and
began tugging at the ropes that held it. At
1:54 in the afternoon, the ropes were set free
and the balloon, bearing the two brave men,
began to lift off the ground.

Captain d'Arlandes thought he should do
something noteworthy for such a special

event. So he whipped out his handkerchief and waved it at the crowd. However, Pilâtre de Rozier apparently thought the captain ought to do some work. "You're not doing anything," he complained, "and we're hardly moving."

"Pardon me," said the captain. He began to feed damp straw and sheep's wool to the fire in the iron pot hanging in the balloon's neck. The balloon slowly rose to a height of nearly three hundred feet (91 m). A gentle wind pushed it along over the rooftops of Paris. Pilâtre de Rozier and d'Arlandes stared down in fascination. They were the first people to look down upon the earth from high in the sky.

However, the men soon had to go to work to keep their balloon from catching fire. Sparks from the burning material in the pot were burning tiny holes in the cloth and paper sides of the balloon. Fortunately, Pilâtre de Rozier and d'Arlandes had brought buckets of water and some sponges with them. Whenever a smoldering hole appeared in the balloon, one of the men would quickly put out the spark with a wet sponge.

But because of the danger, the two fliers let the air in the balloon start to cool. Slowly, the balloon sank back toward the earth and landed in Paris. The first two men to fly had stayed up almost twenty-five minutes. It was a giant step in the conquest of the sky.

Workers filling a balloon
with hydrogen gas in the
early 1800's.

Better balloons

After Pilâtre de Rozier and d'Arlandes
proved that it was safe to go up in a balloon,
many people became interested in balloon
flights. But it was clear that hot air balloons
were not safe—they could easily catch fire
from sparks. There had to be a better way to
keep balloons in the air than to have a fire
burning in them.

Actually, a better way had been found.
Soon after the Montgolfier brothers sent up
their first balloon, a French scientist, Jacques
Charles, made a balloon that used hydrogen
instead of hot air. Hydrogen is a gas that is
lighter than air. By pumping hydrogen into a
balloon, Professor Charles could make the
balloon rise just like a hot-air balloon.

Jacques Charles tested his balloon on August 27, 1783, sending it up from the middle of Paris with hundreds of thousands of people watching. The craft drifted out of sight and came down in a little village some six miles (9.5 kilometers) away. The villagers thought it was a monster and attacked it with guns, swords, and pitchforks.

An old picture (right) showing the flight of the first gas-filled balloon. The first balloon to cross the English Channel (below) had a rudder and four feather-shaped oars of wood and silk.

Nine days after Jean Pilâtre de Rozier and Captain d'Arlandes became the first men to ride a balloon into the sky, Professor Charles and another scientist, Marie-Noël Robert, became the first men to go up in a gas-filled balloon. They rose to a height of 820 feet (25 meters) and drifted about thirty miles (48 km) before coming down.

Gas-filled balloons became known as Charlières, after Professor Charles. More and more people began to build them and try them out. In 1785, Jean-Pierre Blanchard, a Frenchman, and Dr. John Jeffries, an American,

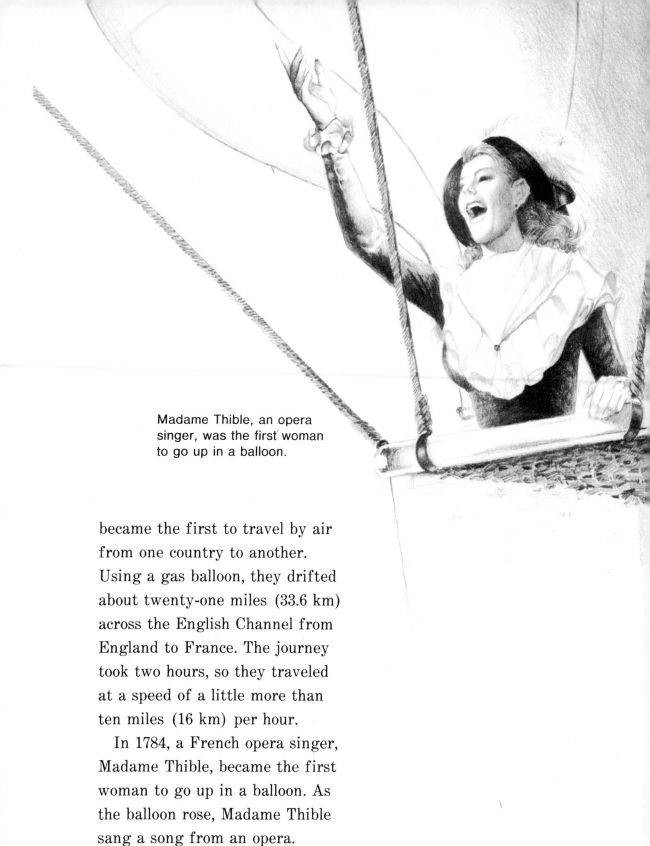

Madame Thible, an opera singer, was the first woman to go up in a balloon.

became the first to travel by air from one country to another. Using a gas balloon, they drifted about twenty-one miles (33.6 km) across the English Channel from England to France. The journey took two hours, so they traveled at a speed of a little more than ten miles (16 km) per hour.

In 1784, a French opera singer, Madame Thible, became the first woman to go up in a balloon. As the balloon rose, Madame Thible sang a song from an opera.

A war balloon

In 1794, eleven years after the Montgolfier brothers sent up the first balloon, France was at war. An Austrian army invaded Belgium, which was then part of France, and a French army hastened to push the Austrians out.

On a hot June day, the Austrians attacked the French army, which had spread out around the town of Charleroi. At first, things went badly for the French, and it looked as if they would be defeated. But then the French called upon their "secret weapon," a balloon named *L'Entreprenant* (*The Daring*).

The balloon was filled with gas and allowed to rise about one thousand feet (300 meters) in the air. Long ropes held it so that it would not drift away. From beneath the huge bag hung a basket large enough to hold two French army officers with telescopes.

The two French officers could see everything the Austrian army was trying to do. They could see where Austrian regiments were being grouped to make an attack, and they could see "weak" places where the Austrians did not have enough men to defend against a French attack. They reported all this information to the French commander, General Jourdan.

Then, wherever the Austrians attacked, they soon found themselves outnumbered by the French soldiers. And swarms of

An old illustration of the first war balloon, *The Daring*. It was used in a battle between France and Austria in 1794.

French soldiers suddenly attacked all the weak Austrian positions.

With the French able to see everything, there was nothing the Austrian general could do but order his army to retreat. In another month, the Austrians left Belgium.

By World War I, a little more than a hundred years later, balloons, airships, and airplanes were being used often in war. But the French balloon *The Daring* was the first "flying machine" to take part in a battle.

A death-defying stunt

On the morning of October 22, 1797, a huge crowd gathered in Monceu Park in Paris. Young André Garnerin had announced he would take off in a balloon, then leave the balloon in midair and fall safely back to earth by means of a special device. Everyone wanted to see if he would really try such a dangerous stunt.

The balloon rose slowly. A huge piece of folded cloth was fastened underneath it. Ropes hanging from this cloth were tied to a large basket in which André Garnerin stood.

The balloon rose higher and higher. People craned their necks to watch it, growing more and more excited.

When the balloon was a little less than a half mile (792 meters) above the ground, Garnerin decided he was high enough. He cut a rope that ran up from the basket to the balloon. Moments later there was a shocked *Ooooh!* from the crowd as they saw that the balloon was still rising, but the basket with Garnerin in it had started to fall. It was no longer attached to the balloon.

Almost at once, the big piece of folded cloth opened up and became a great dome, like a huge umbrella. Instead of falling to earth like a stone, the basket was floating down. Garnerin stood in the basket, triumphantly waving a French flag.

Garnerin had made the world's first
parachute "jump" from an aircraft. He made
many others to entertain crowds, improving
his parachutes so they would float more
slowly and evenly. He proved that parachutes
were safe to use and that they could save
lives.

Make a model parachute

You can make a model parachute that works exactly like a real one. You will need a handkerchief, four pieces of string or heavy thread that are all the same length, and a paper clip or small metal screw.

1. Tie one piece of string or thread to each corner of the handkerchief.

2. Tie the end of each piece of string to the paper clip or screw. Try to keep each piece of string the same length.

3. Gently wad up the handkerchief and strings, keeping the clip or screw on the outside. Throw the wadded-up handkerchief as high into the air as you can. It should open up in the air and drift gently down to the ground, as a real parachute does.

Balloons, Airships, and Flying Machines

The first glider

By the year 1800, balloons had become quite common. It seemed as if the old dream of flying had indeed come true.

But it hadn't, really. For balloons couldn't actually fly, they simply drifted wherever the wind carried them. A true flying machine, one that would go where its pilot wanted it to, had not been invented yet. And most people thought there never would be such a thing.

However, a few people were working on the idea. In 1804, Sir George Cayley, an Englishman, built a small flying machine, a large wing fastened on a long, narrow body. He tested it, and it glided steadily a short distance down the side of a hill.

Cayley's glider was actually the first airplane. But in those days people called it a "heavier-than-air" flying machine because it did not use gas, which is lighter than air, to

hold it up. Cayley's craft was held up by the wind, just as a kite is.

Sir George kept working on his glider. He believed, correctly, that if he could fasten some kind of engine and a propeller to it, the craft could stay in the air. However, no such engine was available then.

About 1852, Cayley built a glider big enough to carry a person. It glided a short distance, carrying a ten-year-old boy as its pilot. That boy, the son of one of Cayley's servants, was the first person to fly in a heavier-than-air flying machine. But, unfortunately, we don't even know his name. Sir George Cayley never bothered to write it down.

Make a model glider

When Sir George Cayley made his model glider, it was the first time anyone had done such a thing. But today, we know a lot more about flying, and anyone can make a glider using a sheet of paper, some transparent tape, and a few paper clips. Here's how:

1. Fold a sheet of notebook paper in half, the long way. Press the fold flat.

2. Open up the sheet and lightly flatten it out. Fold the corners at one end so that the points rest on the center crease. Press the folds flat.

3. Now fold the folded corners in to the center crease. Then fold the sides up along the center crease. Press the folds flat.

4. Now, fold most of each side down to make wings. This will leave a narrow strip at the bottom, between the wings, for the body of the glider. This strip should not be too wide or the wings will not be big enough to make your craft glide.

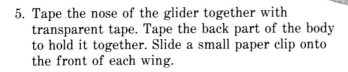

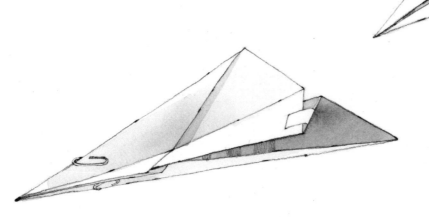

5. Tape the nose of the glider together with transparent tape. Tape the back part of the body to hold it together. Slide a small paper clip onto the front of each wing.

6. Hold the glider at the center of the body, pointed straight ahead, and give it a gentle toss. If you are outside, a gentle breeze blowing from behind will carry the glider for a good distance. You have made a heavier-than-air flying machine of the sort Sir George Cayley made.

An 1843 drawing of the "aerial steam carriage,"
which was never actually built.

The aerial steam carriage

In 1842, an Englishman, William Henson, drew up plans for what he called an "aerial steam carriage." This huge, heavier-than-air flying machine was to have a wing fifty yards (45 meters) long, two enormous propellers, and a large, boatlike body that could hold many passengers. A big steam engine at the rear of the body would supply the power to make the propellers spin.

It was Henson's dream to build a fleet of these flying machines. He hoped to fly passengers and carry mail to all parts of the world. He believed that one of his machines would be able to fly from England to China or India in about twenty-four hours.

However, the aerial steam engine was never built. Henson made a large model that was powered by a small steam engine. He tested the model many times, but it would never fly. Finally, he gave up.

Nevertheless, many people became very interested in this flying machine. Paintings of it sailing through the air appeared in magazines and on towels, dishes, and other items. Stories were written about it.

Although the aerial steam engine was never built, it helped interest others in the idea of building a flying machine. And many of William Henson's ideas were later used by some of these men.

The airship

George Cayley, William Henson, and others believed it would be possible to really fly only with some kind of heavier-than-air machine. But many people still thought that a lighter-than-air machine was the only possible way to fly. They wanted to find some way to power and steer a balloon through the air.

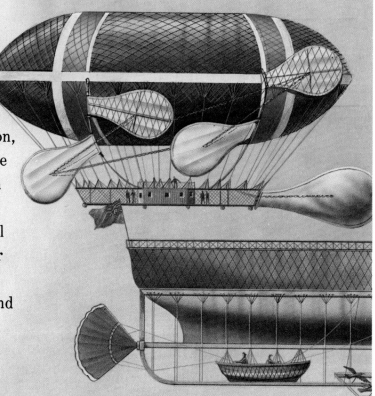

Inventors tried many ways to power and steer balloons. Some tried to row through the air using big paddles; others tried hand-turned propellers. One man even wanted to train birds and harness them to a balloon!

Finally, in 1852, a Frenchman, Henri Giffard, figured out a way that worked. He designed a balloon shaped somewhat like a slim American football. A small steam engine, mounted on a platform beneath the balloon, drove a large propeller.

People had many ideas for powering and steering a balloon. The idea of using big paddles (left) did not work. Neither did the idea of using birds (below) or hand-turned propellers (lower left). But Henri Giffard's idea (lower right) did work. This was the first true airship.

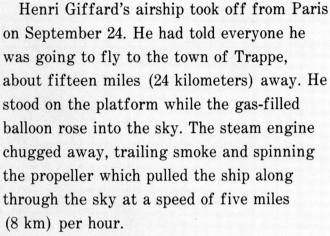

Henri Giffard's airship took off from Paris on September 24. He had told everyone he was going to fly to the town of Trappe, about fifteen miles (24 kilometers) away. He stood on the platform while the gas-filled balloon rose into the sky. The steam engine chugged away, trailing smoke and spinning the propeller which pulled the ship along through the sky at a speed of five miles (8 km) per hour.

The airship flew straight to Trappe, just as Giffard had hoped. He had invented the world's first dirigible (DIHR uh juh buhl or duh RIHJ uh buhl), a lighter-than-air airship that can be steered.

The high flight

Despite Henri Giffard's airship, plain balloons were still the only kind of flying machine most people knew about. And they were quite useful for just going up, not trying to fly to a particular place.

In 1862, an English scientist, James Glaisher, became interested in balloons. Professor Glaisher was a meteorologist, a scientist who studies the air, wind, clouds, and weather. It seemed to him that he might be able to learn a great deal by going up as high as possible in a balloon.

Glaisher hunted around until he found Henry Coxwell, a skilled balloonist who was interested in science. Coxwell thought Glaisher's idea was a good one. He even built a large balloon to take the professor up as high as possible. He named this balloon *Mammoth*.

The two men made a couple of trial trips in the *Mammoth*, just to make sure it worked

properly. Then, on a cloudy September 5,
1862, they loaded Glaisher's equipment and
instruments into the basket and began their
trip.

The balloon soared steadily upward. When
it reached a height of about two miles (3.2
kilometers), it passed through the tops of the
clouds and broke into bright sunshine. It
continued to rise.

After a time, Glaisher checked the
instrument that showed the balloon's height.
It had reached an altitude of 29,500 feet
(8,850 meters), nearly six miles (9.6 km)
above the earth. This was higher than anyone
had ever gone in a balloon. The thermometer
showed a temperature of thirteen degrees
below zero, Fahrenheit (−25° Celsius).

Suddenly, Glaisher found that he couldn't move his arms! His body was numb and he could no longer hold up his head. A moment later, he fainted and fell on his back in the bottom of the basket.

Coxwell also began to feel strange. He realized the balloon was now so high it had reached thin air, and he and Glaisher were not getting enough oxygen. The balloon would have to start back down right away or the two men would be in serious danger!

Coxwell reached for the cord that would open a valve and let gas out of the balloon so it would start down. But the cord had become tangled among the ropes that held the basket to the balloon. Coxwell saw that he would have to climb up the ropes to reach it. Despite the danger involved, he knew he had no choice. But by the time he could reach the cord, his hands were so numb he could not grasp it. He finally leaned forward, took the cord between his teeth, and pulled it by jerking his head.

The balloon began to drop slowly. Coxwell managed to get back down into the basket. As the balloon kept dropping lower, he began to feel better. After a time, Glaisher came to again. The two men landed safely and did not suffer any ill effects from their dangerous adventure.

Glaisher and Coxwell thought their balloon had probably reached a height of nearly seven miles (11.3 km). Most experts now think they did not go that high. But even so, their flight was of great value. Many years later, when other pioneers began to push higher and higher into the sky, they had learned enough from the experience of Glaisher and Coxwell to dress warmly and take containers of oxygen with them.

The balloon airmail

In July 1870, France and Germany went to war. Within two months, the Germans conquered much of France and their army surrounded Paris, the French capital.

The Germans did not want to break into the city as this would cause too much death and destruction. They wanted Paris to surrender. If that happened, they felt that the rest of France would then surrender. To force the surrender, the Germans allowed no one in or out of the city. When the people ran out of food, medicine, and other important things, they would have to give up.

At this time, part of the French government was in Paris and part was in another city in a free area of France. The two parts couldn't communicate, for in those days there were no telephones or radios. And, of course, no mail could get in or out of the city. So the people of Paris didn't know what

was happening in the rest of France, and the rest of France didn't know what was going on in Paris.

Finally, some balloonists living in Paris thought of a way for the city to communicate with other parts of France. They suggested to the head of the French Post Office that letters and messages could be sent out of Paris by means of balloons. The postmaster thought this was a wonderful idea.

A few days later, balloonist Jules Duruof became the first person to carry mail out of the city by air. His balloon came down 56 miles (90 kilometers) away, in safe territory. Two days after that, another balloon soared up and away with a load of mail. And three days later, still another got safely away. But before long, all the balloons that had been in Paris were gone.

However, the postmaster started balloon factories in two railroad stations that were empty because no trains were going in or out of the city. Women were hired to sew pieces of cloth together to form the giant bags. The bags were then coated with varnish to keep gas from leaking out of them, and hung up to

This old illustration shows people making balloons in a railroad station in Paris during 1871.

dry. Finally, ropes and baskets were fastened to them and they were filled with gas and sent floating away.

There were no more trained balloonists left in the city, but a number of men volunteered to pilot the new balloons. They trained for the job by spending hours inside baskets hanging from high places.

Balloons can go only where the wind blows them, so the people that left Paris in balloons did not always come down where they hoped to. Ten balloons floated out of France and landed in Belgium and Holland. Two went the wrong way and came down in Germany, and the pilots became prisoners of war. One went on a nine-hundred-mile (1,540-km) trip across the North Sea and came down in Norway. Two were blown out over the Atlantic Ocean and never seen again.

Naturally, the German generals weren't very happy about all the balloons getting out of Paris. Soldiers were ordered to shoot down any balloons they saw, but they could not hit any. However, German cavalry soldiers did follow some of the balloons until they came down, and then took the pilots prisoner.

France finally surrendered after Paris had been surrounded for 130 days. During that time, sixty-eight balloons had carried more than eleven tons (9.9 metric tons) of mail out of the city. It was history's first airmail service.

The round-trip airship

The airship that Henri Giffard made in 1852
worked pretty well. But it was not very fast
and it could not turn completely around in
the air. People who believed that airships
were the best kind of flying machine knew
there would have to be improvements. They
needed a better engine than the steam
engine. And they had to find a way to steer
an airship so that it could turn around in
flight.

Airmen tried many ideas, but none of them
worked very well. Then in 1884, thirty-two
years after Giffard's airship had flown, two
French army officers built an airship they
named *La France*. It looked like a long,
pointed sausage with a long, narrow boat
hanging under it. A small, light electric

The airship *La France* was the first aircraft that could really fly well.

motor with a large wooden propeller attached to it sat at the front of this boat, or gondola. A large rudder was fastened to the back end of the gondola.

The two soldiers, Captain Charles Renard and Captain Arthur Krebs, tried out their airship for the first time on August 9, 1884. They flew from just outside Paris to the nearby town of Villacoublay, circled that town, and flew back to their starting point. They flew at about fourteen miles (22.4 kilometers) per hour, more than twice as fast as any other airship had ever flown.

The airship *La France* was the first truly successful flying machine. It could go up, come down, steer in a straight line, or turn around in a complete circle. It seemed as if the sky had finally been conquered. Now people could truly fly.

The lost balloon

Airships were still rare in 1897, and there still were no heavier-than-air flying machines. Anyone who wanted to fly could do so only by balloon.

That year, Salomon Andrée, a Swedish explorer and engineer, decided to try to reach the North Pole by air. Other men had tried to reach the pole by crossing the frozen ice of the Arctic Sea, but had failed. Andrée, who had made a number of balloon flights, was sure he could reach the pole in a balloon.

Andrée had a big, specially designed balloon built, which he named *Eagle*. He had invented a steering device that worked pretty well, and had this put on the balloon. On July 11, 1897, Andrée and two helpers, Knut

Fraenkel and Nils Strindberg, took off in the
Eagle from Spitsbergen, an island in the
Arctic Sea. They hoped the wind and
Andrée's steering device would take them
over the pole, some seven hundred miles
(1,120 kilometers) away, and then on to
Russia, where they would land. They had
plenty of food. And they had taken sleds,
snowshoes, hunting rifles, and other
equipment in case they came down and had
to cross the ice on foot.

But they never arrived in Russia. The
three explorers and the giant balloon had
vanished.

This photo, taken by one
of Andrée's helpers, shows
the balloon *Eagle* after it
was forced down onto the
frozen Arctic Ocean.

Fraenkel (left) and Strindberg standing over the polar bear they shot for food.

Thirty-three years went by. Then, in 1930, a group of Norwegian scientists found the bodies of Andrée and Nils Strindberg, together with some equipment and diaries, on a tiny, rocky island in the Arctic Sea. A few days later, searchers found the body of Fraenkel, with more diaries and some rolls of film.

The diaries told what had happened. Andrée had not realized that the warm gas inside the balloon and the bitter cold air outside would cause ice to form quickly on the craft. Coated with ice, the balloon grew heavier and

Two of the doomed explorers, Strindberg (left) and Andrée, at their Arctic camp.

heavier. Despite everything the men could do, it dropped lower and lower, and finally landed. Instead of flying safely over the North Pole, the men were stranded on the frozen ice covering the Arctic Sea.

On foot, they started the long journey back across the ice toward land. They were well equipped, and had a compass with which to find their way. But it was a long trip, and their food ran out. They shot a polar bear, cooked the meat, and ate it. That may have been their undoing, for the bear had been diseased and the men became sick and died.

The rolls of film were developed and they produced fine pictures that the men had taken on the journey across the ice. Their bodies were taken home to Sweden and buried with honors.

The daring dirigible pilot

No one living in Paris in 1900 was ever
surprised to see a small airship "parked" in
the street beside a restaurant. They knew at
once that Alberto Santos-Dumont was in that
restaurant having lunch.

Alberto Santos-Dumont was a rich young
Brazilian who lived in France. He became
interested in airships in 1897 and began

building his own. In 1898, he went up in his
first airship, *Dirigible Number One*, and was
nearly killed. But he simply built *Dirigible
Number Two* and went up in it in 1899. Over
several years, he built a total of fourteen.
Each one was an improvement over the
previous one.

Santos-Dumont had a number of exciting
and dangerous adventures in his dirigibles.
One time, the engine caught fire in the air.
Santos-Dumont calmly put out the fire by
smothering it with his straw hat. Another

time, the balloon part of the airship collapsed in midair, and the ship started to fall. But it fell only a short distance, landing on the roof of a house in Paris. Still another time, one of his dirigibles landed in a tree.

Santos-Dumont was fond of flying his airships over Paris, and people grew quite accustomed to the sight. Most of his dirigibles were fairly small, and he would often land on the street, "parking" next to a restaurant while he had lunch or dinner. There were no cars on the streets in those days, and no laws about parking.

Most airships still could not be steered very well at this time. It was generally difficult to make them turn around quickly in the air. In 1900, a wealthy French businessman offered a large cash prize to any airship flyer who could circle the Eiffel Tower in Paris. To win, the airship had to take off from the nearby town of Saint Cloud, fly to Paris, circle the tower, and fly back to Saint Cloud, all within thirty minutes.

This photograph, taken in 1901, shows Alberto Santos-Dumont flying one of his airships around the Eiffel Tower in Paris.

A number of pilots tried for the prize and failed. Santos-Dumont did not care about the money, but he wanted to show how well his dirigibles could fly.

He tried for the prize once, and failed as all the others had. But on October 19, 1901, he tried again, and won. His *Dirigible Number 6* came from Saint Cloud, flew in a tight little circle around the Eiffel Tower, and made it back to Saint Cloud in exactly $29\frac{1}{2}$ minutes.

The airship flights made by Alberto Santos-Dumont convinced many people that flying was not just a silly dream, but could be a wonderful and useful means of transportation.

An airship with a skeleton

While young Alberto Santos-Dumont was building airships in France, a much older man in Germany was trying to build a better airship than anyone had yet been able to make. He was Count Ferdinand von Zeppelin, a German nobleman.

In 1898, the sixty-year-old Count von Zeppelin began spending huge sums of money to build a rigid (stiff) airship. Instead of a thin bag filled with gas, like other airships, his craft had a metal frame, a skeleton, with a cloth "skin" stretched over it. He stored the gas in compartments inside the frame. Thus, this kind of airship could never

lose its shape as the other kind did when gas
was let out of them.

Count von Zeppelin himself piloted his new
airship on its first test flight in 1900. It rose
more than one thousand feet (1,600 kilometers)
and stayed in the air for twenty minutes.

By 1908, Count von Zeppelin had built
three more rigid airships, each better than
the last. They became known as zeppelins,
and they all looked like huge sausages
floating in the air. Some butcher shops in
Germany still sell a long sausage called a
zeppelinwurst, which got its name because it
looks like one of Count Zeppelin's airships.

Later, rigid airships were built in several
other countries. They, too, were called zeppelins.

The Coming
of the Airplane

The boy who wanted to fly

It was almost midnight, and the little town of Anklam, Germany, lay dark and silent in the moonlight. Not a soul stirred in the shadowed streets. Everyone was asleep.

No—not everyone. Out on the broad meadow beyond the town, two small boys were running through the tall grass. One of them had a broad, thin, wooden board strapped to each arm. As he ran, he flapped his arms as if he were trying to fly.

As a matter of fact, that is exactly what he was trying to do. The two boys were brothers, Otto and Gustav Lilienthal.

Thirteen-year-old Otto thought he had figured out how to fly by strapping artificial wings on his arms. But this was 1873, and the idea of a person trying to fly, except in a balloon or airship, seemed funny to most people. Otto did not want to be laughed at, so he and Gustav waited until everyone in Anklam was asleep, then sneaked out to try the wings in secret.

The wings did not work, of course. But as Otto Lilienthal grew up, he never lost his dream of flying. In those days, airships—lighter-than-air craft—were becoming more common. But Otto believed that a heavier-than-air craft, with wings, would be best. He dreamed of building such a machine that could carry him through the air.

Over the years, Otto studied birds to learn how their wings worked. He built many small models of winged flying machines and tested them. Slowly, he learned how to make a winged machine that could glide like a soaring bird.

By 1891, when he was thirty-one years old, Otto Lilienthal decided he was ready to try to fly. He built a gliding machine that was big enough to carry a man. It consisted mainly of a pair of big wings made of cotton cloth stretched over thin strips of bamboo. The glider was light enough for a man to carry, but strong enough to hold a man's weight.

Holding the glider with the big wings

Otto Lilienthal made more than two thousand flights with glider wings like these.

spreading out above him, Otto ran along the ground to gain speed. He had built a kind of springboard, and when he reached it, he sprang into the air. He was moving fast enough so that the air lifted up the big wings, and the glider skimmed along above the ground with Otto hanging from it. At last, he knew how it felt to soar through the sky like a bird.

As time went on, Otto built other gliders and made more than two thousand flights. At times, he traveled 750 feet (225 meters) or more through the air, high above the ground. He designed and installed a movable tail on his glider, so that he could control the direction of his flight. He began to work on the idea of putting a motor on a winged flying machine, so it could get off the ground by itself and stay in the air.

Others interested in heavier-than-air flying machines heard about Lilienthal's work, and some came to learn from him. He became famous.

Then something went wrong on a glider flight one August day in 1896. The glider fell fifty feet (15 m) and smashed into the ground. Otto Lilienthal's back was broken, and he died a day later.

But other people began to use all the knowledge Otto Lilienthal had gained from his flights and his ideas about how to build flying machines. His work helped other men build the heavier-than-air flying machines that later conquered the sky.

Otto Lilienthal testing a two-winged glider.

Two wings are better than one

The United States, too, had a "glider man."
He was Octave Chanute, an engineer and
bridgebuilder. He heard of Otto Lilienthal's
experiments with gliders and became
interested in the idea of flying. Chanute
began building gliders in 1896, the year
Lilienthal was killed. But he felt that
Lilienthal's gliders might have worked better
if they had had more than one wing. One of
Chanute's first gliders had six pairs of

This 1896 photograph shows Octave Chanute's helper A. M. Herring making a flight on the two-winged glider that Chanute designed.

wings. He used his knowledge of bridge-building to construct the wings and hold them together.

However, Chanute quickly began cutting down on the number of wings he put on his gliders. He went from six pairs to three, and then from three to two. Chanute was in his sixties, so he did not fly any of his gliders himself. However, he had several young assistants who made more than two thousand glides on the two-winged glider. It was so well built and worked so well that they never had an accident with it.

The two-winged glider became known as the Chanute glider. It was important because it gave other men who were interested in flying some good ideas.

Fantastic flying machines

At about the same time Lilienthal and Chanute were working with gliders, a few other men were trying to build flying machines that could fly under their own power.

In 1894, in England, inventor Hiram Maxim built a huge machine that had wings 103 feet (30 meters) long. It had propellers the size of windmills that were powered by big steam engines. Maxim's plane required a crew of three to operate all of the controls. However, this big machine never flew. Maxim simply ran it around on the ground and never even tried to take off.

In 1894, inventor Hiram Maxim built a gigantic flying machine that never left the ground.

In 1897, Clement Ader of France built a flying machine that looked a little like a giant bat. He, too, used a steam engine for power. But all this machine could do was hop along on the ground.

Clement Ader's 1897 flying machine had batlike wings but could not fly.

In 1896, American astronomer and physicist Samuel Langley built a model flying machine that was powered by a steam engine. It flew quite well, so Langley built a full-sized machine that could carry a man and was powered by a gasoline engine. He called this machine an "aerodrome."

Langley planned to test his aerodrome by having a pilot fly it off the roof of a houseboat in the middle of the Potomac River. But on the first test in 1903, it just dived into the water. The machine broke apart and fell into the water again on the second test. The pilot was rescued both times.

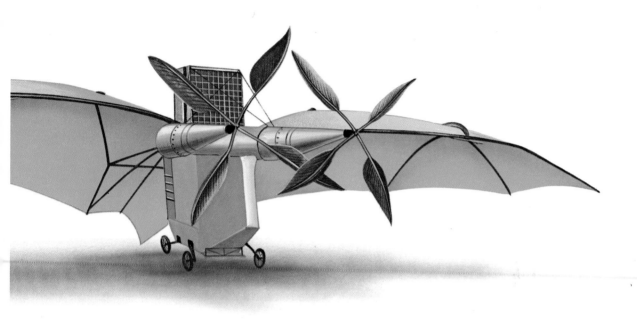

Samuel Langley's flying machine fell into the Potomac River.

The first airplane

While Maxim, Langley, and others were trying to build flying machines, Wilbur and Orville Wright of Dayton, Ohio, became interested in flying. The brothers owned a small bicycle factory and were used to tinkering with machines and building things.

Wilbur and Orville read about Otto Lilienthal's work. In 1899, they began building gliders and flying on them as Lilienthal had done. But they used some new ideas of their own to make the gliders stay in the air longer and to make them easier to control. They worked out ways to make their gliders go up and down and turn right or left in the air.

The two took turns making hundreds of flights in gliders, and they learned how to control a two-winged glider perfectly. At last they decided they knew enough. They were ready to try to fly in a glider that would move under its own power, instead of depending on the wind to make it move. They would build a glider with propellers and with an engine that could make the propellers spin.

They decided that a gasoline engine would be the best kind to use on their flying machine. However, they had to have a very small, light engine, and no one made such an engine. But Wilbur and Orville, fine mechanics, built their own engine, hooking it up to the two propellers they also made.

Their flying machine was a strange, rickety-looking thing made of cloth, strips of wood, and wire. It was nothing more than two pairs of big wings, one above the other, with the tiny engine and the two propellers

Wilbur Wright testing one of the Wright brothers' gliders. Such tests helped them work out the ideas for their airplane.

attached. The pilot had to lie on his stomach on the bottom wing.

Wilbur and Orville took this machine, called *Flyer*, to Kitty Hawk, in North Carolina, where they made all their glider flights. This was a broad, flat, sandy place with no trees, where a strong wind was almost always blowing.

The brothers put down a sixty-foot (18-meter) wooden track as a runway from which their flying machine would take off. *Flyer* had to move along the ground until it gained enough speed to lift into the air, but it had no wheels. It simply rested on a wheeled platform that rolled along the track. When *Flyer* started to take off, the platform would roll along under it until it lifted into the air.

On the morning of December 14, 1903, the brothers felt they were ready to make the first test. They flipped a coin to see who would be the pilot. Wilbur won the toss. But when he tried to take off, the machine slipped off the track and was slightly damaged.

After making repairs, Wilbur and Orville decided to try again on the morning of December 17. This time, Orville would be the pilot.

It was a cold, gray day, with a chill north wind. A thin skin of ice covered the little puddles of water that dotted the ground.

Flyer's little engine was started and

This is an actual photograph of one of the greatest events in history—the first airplane flight, on December 17, 1903.

Orville crawled onto the wing. "All set," he called to his brother.

"Let her go," shouted Wilbur.

Orville unfastened the wire that held the machine. Its propellers whirring, *Flyer* began to roll slowly along the track. Wilbur ran alongside for a few steps, steadying one wing with his hand. Then the machine picked up speed and surged forward. Two-thirds of the way along the track, it lifted into the air.

Peering down, Orville saw the ground slipping swiftly past, ten feet (3 m) beneath him. He was flying—the first man to fly in an engine-powered, heavier-than-air flying machine, the kind we now call an airplane.

The machine flew for about twelve seconds,
at a speed of thirty miles (48 kilometers) per
hour. It was not a smooth flight. *Flyer* rose
and fell in the air as if it were coasting on
ocean waves. But it landed gently, about 120
feet (37 m) from where it had started.
Orville slid off the wing and stood up.

"We did it, Will," he said happily, as his
brother came running up.

Wilbur and Orville made three more flights
that day, taking turns as pilot. The last one
lasted nearly a full minute and went 852 feet
(260 m).

Four men and a sixteen-year-old boy from
Kitty Hawk were on hand to watch, and one

of them took a photograph of *Flyer* rising into the air. Yet, when the Wright brothers announced that they had flown, most people did not believe them. Very few realized what an important thing had happened.

What made the Wright brothers' flight so much more important than the flight of a balloon, airship, or a glider? *Flyer* took off under its own power, pulled upward by its whirling propellers. It did not have to depend upon hot air, gas, or wind to lift it off the ground. It also flew steadily in a straight line without being helped or hindered by the wind. It proved that a heavier-than-air machine could fly under its own power, carrying a person, which most people had thought was impossible.

That day in 1903 was one of the most important days in history. The sky had truly been conquered at last. The first airplane had flown.

The man who was ahead of his time

Even at the very moment Orville Wright was making the first flight in a heavier-than-air machine, most people still believed that no one could ever fly except in a balloon or airship. Only a few people thought it would be possible for a heavier-than-air machine to fly, and they were thinking far ahead of most others. But there was at least one person who was thinking even further ahead than they were.

Even before the Wright brothers built the first airplane that was to fly, Konstantin Tsiolkovsky, a Russian schoolteacher, was thinking about flying in space. In 1897, he worked out the idea of using a rocket engine to launch a spaceship. He also designed rockets and developed ideas of how spacecraft could leave and re-enter the earth's atmosphere.

Tsiolkovsky's ideas were far ahead of their time. Most people were not even thinking about flying in the sky at that time. So, for a long time, no one paid much attention to his ideas about flying in space.

Today, many scientists feel that Tsiolkovsky was the "father" of space flight—the first person to find answers to many of the problems that had to be solved before human beings could go into space.

Konstantin Tsiolkovosky, a Russian physics teacher, was the first to state the correct theory of rocket power.

Make a model rocket ship

Konstantin Tsiolkovsky knew a rocket engine would work in space, because the force that shoots out of the back of a rocket creates a *thrust* that drives the rocket forward no matter where it is. You can see how this thrust works by making a model rocket from a balloon, a plastic or paper soda straw, some string, and some heavy paper. You will also need scissors.

1. Cut off about one-third of the soda straw. Slide this section of the soda straw about halfway into the open end of the balloon.

2. With the string, tie the end of the balloon firmly around the soda straw. Do not tie it so tightly that the straw is pinched shut, however.

3. Cut a small rectangle of paper about two inches by four inches (5 x 10 centimeters) in size. Fold this in half, then open it up. In the center of the rectangle, right on the creased line, poke a small hole with the scissors.

4. Then, slide the hole over the end of the soda straw sticking out of the balloon. Press the two folds of the paper together again, slightly. This is the tail of your rocket.

5. Fill the balloon full of air by blowing into the soda straw. Press your thumb over the end of the straw to keep the air from escaping, and point the balloon in the direction you want it to go. Take your thumb off the end of the straw. The air will rush out of the balloon, creating a thrust that will make the balloon shoot forward. This is exactly how a real rocket works. And your model would actually work in space, too.

Airplanes everywhere

In this airplane, Alberto Santos-Dumont, the famous airship builder, made the first airplane flight in Europe, in 1907.

After their successful flights in 1903, the Wright brothers kept on flying and learning new things about flight. They kept changing their airplane so it would perform better. By the end of 1905, a Wright brothers airplane could fly as far as twenty-four miles (38 kilometers), turn in any direction, and even fly in a circle.

By this time, no one was making fun of airplanes anymore. Now that the Wright brothers had shown how, many other people began trying to build airplanes, too.

The first man to fly an airplane in Europe was none other than Alberto Santos-Dumont, the airship builder. He built an airplane in

France and tried it out in 1906. It was a strange-looking craft that had its tail in front and looked as if it were made of box kites. But it flew nearly two hundred feet (about 60 meters) on its first test flight.

Throughout Europe, inventors began testing airplanes they had built. Most of these looked much like the Wright or Santos-Dumont airplanes. But in 1907, a Frenchman, Paul Cornu, built a wingless aircraft that had two huge propellers pointed up at the sky instead of straight ahead. When Cornu turned on the engine and the

In 1907, Paul Cornu of France built the world's first successful helicopter.

Henri Farman, of France, in the airplane in which he made the first "long-distance" flight in Europe, in 1908.

propellers started to spin, they lifted the machine one foot (0.3 m) off the ground. Cornu's craft was the world's first helicopter.

By this time, the Wright brothers were making flights that lasted as long as an hour. But no one in Europe had flown more than a few minutes. Then, in 1908, Henri Farman, an Englishman who lived in France, made the first "long-distance" flight in Europe. He flew $16\frac{1}{2}$ miles (26.5 km) from one French town to another in an airplane built by two brothers, Gabriel and Charles Voisin. The flight took about twenty minutes.

So, by the beginning of 1909, long-distance flights over land were becoming fairly common. But no one had yet made a long-distance flight over water.

Many of the early airplanes, such as the two shown here, simply did not work.

Why we call them "airplanes"

Why did the Wright brothers call their flying machine an *"airplane"*?

The word *plane* means a "flat surface." A tabletop is a plane. A smooth wall is a plane. And each of the long, flat wings that formed the Wright brothers' flying machine was a plane. Inasmuch as these were planes that moved through the air, people called them "airplanes."

The first airplanes were known by the number of pairs of wings, or planes, they had. A craft with two wings was called a "biplane"—the word *bi* means "two." A craft with three wings was known as a "triplane." *Tri* means "three." A craft with only one wing was a "monoplane." The word *mono* means "one."

biplane

triplane

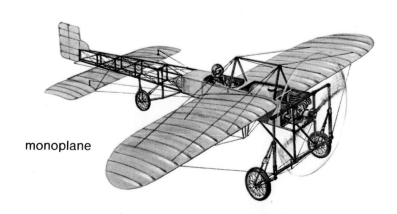

monoplane

The challenge of the channel

The English Channel is the strip of sea that lies between France and England. At its narrowest point it is about twenty-two miles (35 kilometers) wide. In 1909, an English newspaper, the London *Daily Mail*, offered a reward to the first person to fly an airplane either way across the channel.

This was a dangerous challenge. Airplane engines did not work well and they might fail in the middle of a flight. On a flight over land, the pilot had a chance to land safely if something went wrong, but a plane forced down on water might sink and the pilot might drown. However, a few flyers were willing to risk their lives—not only for the reward, but also for the fame of being the first to make such a historic flight.

The first to try was Hubert Latham of France. He took off on July 19 from the coast of France in an airplane known as an Antoinette. However, the Antoinette's engine stopped only a short way out over the channel. Latham managed to land the plane smoothly on the water, where it floated. Luckily, a French ship was nearby, and rescued him.

On July 25, French pilot Louis Blériot set out in *Blériot XI*, a craft he had built himself. He took off at about 4:30 in the

morning from a field on the French coast, at
the narrowest part of the channel. A French
navy ship followed him for a time.

At first, all went well. Blériot stayed only
a few feet (about 1.5 meters) above the
water, so that if anything went wrong he
would not have far to drop. However, the
sight of the waves rising and falling so close
to him made Blériot faintly seasick.

It was a hazy day. After about ten
minutes, Blériot turned his head to see if the
warship were still following. But he could not
see it, and he could no longer see the French
coastline. He seemed to be all alone, flying
through a gray haze, above the gray waves.

After another ten minutes, Blériot became
slightly worried. He had not yet sighted the

coast of England. He did not have a compass, so he was not sure that he was still heading in the right direction. If the airplane had turned slightly, without his noticing it, he might be heading straight out to sea. If so, he would soon run out of gasoline and the airplane would drop into the water.

To make matters worse, Blériot realized that the engine was beginning to get much too hot. This was dangerous, because the airplane could catch fire. But Blériot could do nothing but grimly keep flying, praying that he would soon reach the English coast.

The engine grew hotter, and smoke curled up from it. But then, in a sudden, wonderful stroke of luck, rain began to fall. A torrent of cold water pelted the engine, quickly cooling it down. Blériot heaved a sigh of relief.

A short time later, he saw the white cliffs of the English coast gleaming in the distance. He turned the plane's nose upward to gain altitude and flew over the cliffs. The green landscape of England spread out beneath him. He headed for a broad meadow that lay at the foot of a stately gray castle and guided his craft down to a landing. The flight had taken about 37 minutes.

A crowd of excited people soon gathered around the Frenchman and his plane. To these people, Blériot's flight was as wonderful as the first flight to the moon

Harriet Quimby, an American, was the first woman to fly across the English Channel.

would be for people many years later. He was the first person to cross a large body of water in an airplane. And he had risked his life to do so.

However, other pilots quickly followed in Blériot's footsteps. In 1910, two Americans and a pet cat flew across the channel from France to England, and an English pilot flew across from England to France and back, without stopping. In 1912, Harriet Quimby, an American, became the first woman to fly across the channel.

All these flights showed that air travel brought countries that had always seemed far apart much closer together. Many people now realized that airplanes were going to change the world.

the Henri Fabre seaplane

the Curtiss flying boat

Bigger, better, faster

Louis Blériot was prepared in case his
airplane went down in the sea. He took along
a big air-filled bag that would have kept him
afloat until a boat came along to rescue him.
But in 1910, another Frenchman, Henri
Fabre, built an airplane that could "land" on,
and take off from, water. The first seaplane,
it had floats instead of wheels.

Then in 1911, American inventor Glenn
Curtiss built a plane that had a light boat for
its body. He tested this craft in January 1912.
It sailed along on the water and then took off
into the air—the world's first flying boat.

the Deperdussin
monoplane

At this time, most planes could not go
much faster than fifty or sixty miles (80-96
kilometers) per hour. In 1912, Chicago held a
big international air race. One of the planes
entered in the race was a beautiful,
streamlined craft with a body shaped like a
fish. It was built by Armand Deperdussin of

France. This plane won the race easily, becoming the first airplane to fly at more than one hundred miles (160 km) per hour.

Up until 1913, most airplanes had one, or at the most two, engines. But in 1913, Russian inventor Igor Sikorsky built a huge, two-winged plane that had four engines and a closed passenger cabin. The cabin contained four seats and a sofa, as well as a washroom and a clothes closet.

Airplanes were getting bigger, better, and faster. But in 1914, Europe was on the verge of war—a war that would affect most of the world. And airplanes and airships would play a big part in it.

the Sikorsky
four-engine biplane

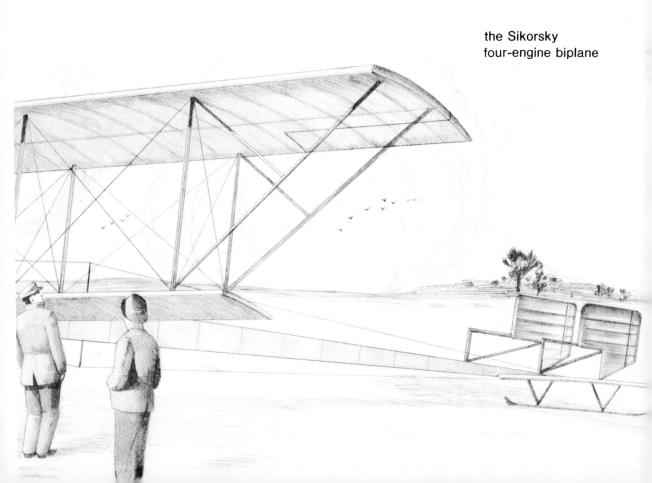

War in the Air

Fighting airplanes

World War I began in July 1914, and went on
for more than four years. On one side were
the Allies—Belgium, France, Great Britain,
Russia, and, later, Italy, the United States,
and other nations. On the other side were the
Central Powers—Austria-Hungary, Bulgaria,
Germany, and Turkey.

There was no such thing as a warplane when the war began. All of the armies had some airplanes, but they were just ordinary airplanes. Generals thought that these planes were best suited for scouting and spying. So, pilots would fly over enemy territory and try to find out such information as where cannons were hidden and where troops were positioned. Thus, airplanes became known as "the eyes of the army."

French Morane Saulnier

German Gotha Taube (Dove)

The first planes used in World War I had no weapons, but the pilots sometimes shot at each other with pistols!

However, the pilots were all soldiers and most of them wanted to fight for their country. So, many of them started to carry small bombs, or even bags of bricks, to drop on enemy soldiers! Some carried rifles and pistols with which to shoot at enemy airplanes they encountered. It did not take the generals long to see that it would be useful if airplanes could fight. For one thing, they could shoot down enemy scout planes so that they could not gather information.

The British army built the first real warplane in 1915. It was an airplane made especially for fighting. Called the Gunbus, it had a machine gun fastened to its front. Soon, every nation at war was building such planes. And each one tried to make planes that were faster and better than anything the enemy had.

By 1918, the last year of the war, most of the warring nations had thousands of fast, well-built warplanes of several kinds. In addition to observation planes,

The Vickers Gunbus was the first airplane built especially for war. It had a machine gun mounted at the front.

French Voisin bomber

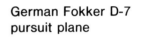

German Fokker D-7
pursuit plane

British SE5A
pursuit plane

used for spying on the enemy, there were now also pursuit planes, whose job it was to chase enemy planes and shoot them down. And there were big four-engine bombers that could carry dozens of big bombs to drop on distant targets.

World War I was the first war in history in which airplanes were used in the fighting. But from then on, warplanes became a very important part of every nation's armed forces.

Dogfight!

The gray light of dawn was beginning to color the sky above a broad field in France on a spring morning in 1917. Six Nieuport 17 biplanes sat in a row on the field, their wings and sides marked with the blue, white, and red emblem of the British Royal Flying Corps. Groups of mechanics moved around each plane making last-minute checks.

In the distance stood a large, grand building with many towers, turrets, and windows. It had once been the home of a wealthy French nobleman. Now, it was home for a number of British pilots, mechanics, and others who tended the twenty some airplanes that formed what was known as a pursuit squadron.

A number of motorcycles came buzzing from the building toward the row of

Nieuports. Each motorcycle had a sidecar in which a man rode. The motorcycles rolled to a stop near the planes and the men climbed out of the sidecars. They were dressed in heavy leather coats with fur collars and fur-lined leather helmets, and each man wore or carried a pair of goggles. These were the pilots who would fly the Nieuports on that day's dawn patrol.

The officer in command walked to the first plane in the row and climbed into the cockpit. A mechanic moved to the front of the plane and stood before the propeller. "Good morning, sergeant," said the pilot.

"A very good day to you, sir," said the mechanic. "Switch off, sir?"

The pilot checked his control panel. "Switch off."

The mechanic raised his hands and gripped the propeller. "Switch on," he called.

The pilot flicked a switch on the panel. "Switch on," he called back.

"Contact," barked the mechanic. Then with all his strength, he swung the propeller downward and quickly stepped back. The Nieuport's engine coughed and broke into a deep roar, and the propeller became a shimmer of spinning motion.

The flight commander looked down the row of planes and saw that all the other propellers were spinning. He raised an arm, and each of the other pilots raised an arm to

show they were ready. Lowering his arm, the
commander gunned his engine and began to
taxi forward. One after another, the other
planes followed. Faster and faster, the six
aircraft sped across the field, their tails
lifting, until they gained enough air speed to
lift completely off the ground.

The six planes climbed into the sky at a
gentle angle until the farmland beneath them
looked like a green and brown checkerboard
in the brightening daylight. Then the
commander set his plane on its course and
the others followed. The patrol had begun.

As he flew, the commander's eyes never
stopped moving. He peered down at the earth

from both sides of the cockpit, turned his head from side to side to search the surrounding sky and stared upward at the sky overhead. After a time, he spotted what he had been watching for. In the distance, off to one side and several hundred feet lower than the British planes, five enemy aircraft were approaching from the opposite direction. By the shape of their wings and their pointed noses, the commander

recognized them as Albatross D.III's, German
fighter planes.

The British planes were strung out in a
diagonal line no more than ten or fifteen
yards (9 or 13.5 meters) apart. The commander
waved his arm to attract the attention of the
pilot of the nearest plane and pointed toward
the Germans. The other nodded and relayed
the signal to the man nearest to him. Within
seconds, each British flier was aware of the
oncoming enemy.

The commander yanked the cocking levers
of the two machine guns mounted in front of
the cockpit. He fired a short burst from each
gun to make sure they were not jammed.
Then he shoved the control stick forward,
pushing the right rudder pedal with his foot,
and nosed over in a long, curving dive toward
the German planes that were now climbing
toward him. The other British planes
followed close behind.

When the two patrols met, they quickly
broke up into a confusing whirl of darting,
dodging, climbing, diving shapes. Each pilot
tried to get into position to shoot at an
enemy plane while trying to keep from being
shot at himself.

The British commander had picked out the
plane he believed was piloted by the German
commander. It was brightly colored, with a
red nose, yellow body, and blue tail. The
Englishman tried to stay with the German

plane as it veered, twisted, and dodged. The German pilot flew skillfully and the Englishman simply could not get a good shot at the plane.

Then the Englishman saw a line of bullet holes suddenly pop out on the cloth of his lower right wing. Jerking his head around, he saw that another German plane had managed

to get behind him. Little flashes of light twinkled above its nose as its two machine guns spurted bullets at his plane.

The Englishman kicked his rudder pedal, causing his plane to skid abruptly to one side. The surprised German flashed past him, and instantly the Englishman had his Nieuport on the Albatross's tail. For a few moments the

enemy plane was dead in the center of the
sight between the Englishman's two machine
guns and he immediately opened fire,
sending streams of bullets into it. The
Albatross seemed to jerk and belched a puff
of dark, oily smoke. Then, smoke trailing
from it, it began to fall toward the ground in
a long slanting dive.

At once, the Englishman anxiously scanned
the sky all around him, concerned that
another enemy plane might have slipped in
behind him. But the sky now seemed empty.
Far in the distance—too far to chase—a
German plane was speeding away, close to

the ground, but no other planes could be seen.

The Englishman knew that once a dogfight began, it quickly spread out. Planes went in all directions as they chased, or were chased by, enemy aircraft. By now, the other pilots in his patrol were far apart.

There was nothing to do but head back to the home airfield. The commander knew that all of his men would do the same, if they were alive and still flying. He hoped they would all get back safely, but he knew he might never see some of them again. For after every dogfight, there were always one or two men who never came back.

Legion of Honor
(France)

Men called "aces"

As soon as nations armed airplanes with machine guns in World War I, it became the job of many pilots to try to shoot down enemy planes. Air battles became common.

However, it was not easy to shoot down another plane—the pilot had to be a very good flier, a very good shot, and very lucky. A pilot who shot down two or three planes was doing quite well. And any man who shot down five planes was something special. He was known as an "ace."

But there were some aces who shot down a lot more than five planes—thirty, fifty, and even more. These aces became great heroes in their own countries, and many won the respect and admiration of their enemies. Many aces had nicknames and flew in specially colored or decorated airplanes, so everyone would know who they were. They were much like knights of old, risking their lives every day by going out and fighting duels against the enemy.

Many World War I aces were decorated with medals such as these for their bravery.

Victoria Cross
(Great Britain)

Iron Cross, Second Class
(Germany)

One of the most famous aces was a German pilot, Baron Manfred von Richthofen. He shot down the most planes of any pilot in World War I—eighty. Baron von Richthofen almost always flew a plane that was painted all red or at least partly red, and was known as ''the Red Baron.'' He commanded a group of fighter pilots who all flew brightly colored airplanes and were known as ''Richthofen's Flying Circus.''

The next highest ranking ace was Captain René Fonck, a Frenchman who shot down seventy-five German planes. Once, he attacked three German planes at the same time and shot down all three in less than a minute. Captain Fonck was a member of a famous French pilot group, ''the Storks.''

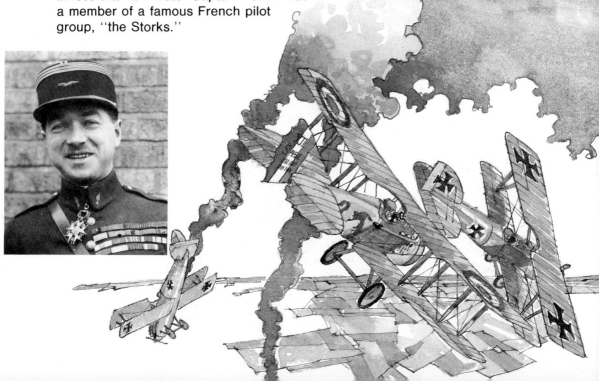

England's Major Edward Mannock was next in line, with seventy-three victories. And right behind him, with seventy-two was Major Billy Bishop, a Canadian. Bishop once attacked a German airfield alone. Three planes flew up to fight him, and he shot them all down.

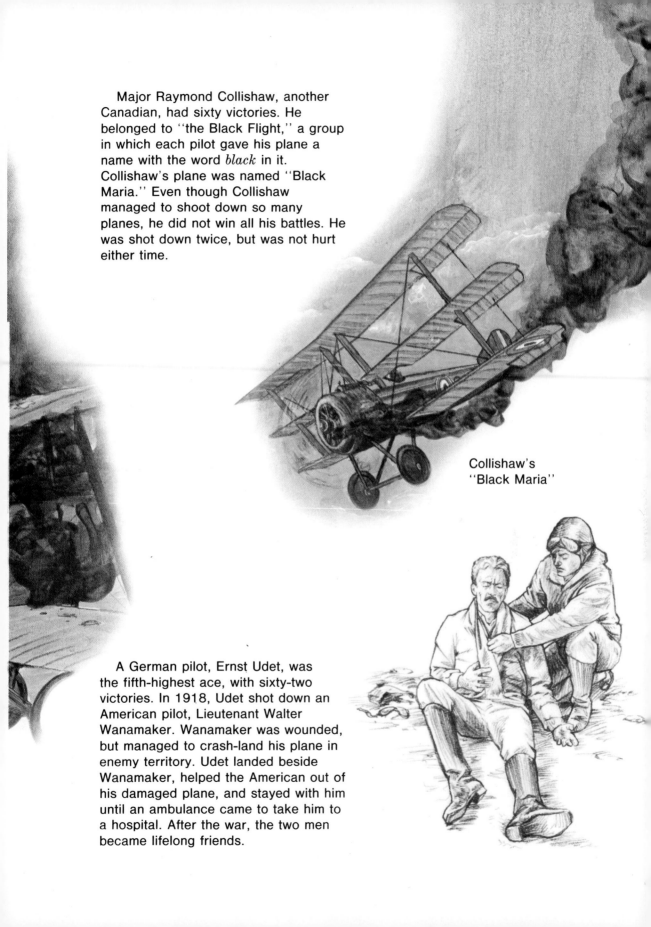

Major Raymond Collishaw, another Canadian, had sixty victories. He belonged to "the Black Flight," a group in which each pilot gave his plane a name with the word *black* in it. Collishaw's plane was named "Black Maria." Even though Collishaw managed to shoot down so many planes, he did not win all his battles. He was shot down twice, but was not hurt either time.

Collishaw's "Black Maria"

A German pilot, Ernst Udet, was the fifth-highest ace, with sixty-two victories. In 1918, Udet shot down an American pilot, Lieutenant Walter Wanamaker. Wanamaker was wounded, but managed to crash-land his plane in enemy territory. Udet landed beside Wanamaker, helped the American out of his damaged plane, and stayed with him until an ambulance came to take him to a hospital. After the war, the two men became lifelong friends.

France's Captain Georges Guynemer shot down fifty-four planes and was shot down seven times himself. On the day after his fifty-fourth victory, he flew off and was never seen again. No one knows what happened to him.

Lieutenant Charles Nungesser, a Frenchman who shot down forty-five planes, flew a plane that was decorated with a white skull and crossbones inside a black heart. He was wounded and injured many times, and often had to be carried to his plane because he was too crippled to walk.

Lieutenant Charles Nungesser

There were many other famous World War I aces. An Englishman, Major James McCudden, shot down a total of fifty-seven planes. Another Englishman, Captain Albert Ball, shot down forty-four planes. He once attacked five German planes by himself, shooting down two of them.

Captain Albert Ball

Captain Edward Rickenbacker

The United States did not enter World War I until 1917, so American fliers did not have as much time to score victories as many of the European pilots did. The top American ace was Captain Eddie Rickenbacker, who shot down twenty-six aircraft in eight months of combat. Rickenbacker belonged to the American 94th Aero Squadron. Its symbol was Uncle Sam's red, white, and blue hat, inside a red ring.

British SE5A

German Halberstadt CL II

Air raids

Scores of searchlight beams reached up into the black night sky over London. They moved restlessly, criss-crossing and forming pale spiderwebs in the sky. Suddenly, one of them caught something, and a second beam swung over to add its light. Through their pale shafts slid a huge, long shape like a gigantic silver cigar. In the city streets, people stared up in fear. The zeppelins had come! It was an air raid!

World War I was the first war to have air raids—attacks on cities by airships or airplanes dropping bombs. During the war,

This German zeppelin, damaged over England, was shot down by French antiaircraft fire.

Paris was bombed more than fifty times and London was bombed twenty-one times. Some German cities were also bombed.

Some of the most frightening air raids were made by zeppelins, the huge airships built by Count von Zeppelin of Germany. From 1915 to 1917, London was bombed twelve times by zeppelins. They always came at night, and there were usually several of them. Searchlights would hunt for them, and when they were seen, antiaircraft guns would begin to fire. The thud of exploding shells and the boom of bombs startled people out of their sleep.

London, Paris, and some Italian cities were also bombed by fleets of huge airplanes known as Gotha bombers. World War I's air raids brought a new terror into the world. People knew that never again would any city be safe from aircraft dropping bombs.

Sky spies
and sky fences

Balloons were used in World War I
both for keeping an eye on the
enemy, and for fashioning a
"fence" in the sky to keep out
enemy aircraft.

Observation, or "lookout" balloons
were fastened to the ground with
long cables, close to enemy territory.
They were allowed to rise as far
into the sky as the cable would let
them, usually thousands of feet
(meters). A soldier in a basket
hanging beneath the balloon could
see far into enemy territory. If he
saw something important he would
telephone to his commanding
officers on the ground and report
what he had seen.

Of course, none of the armies
wanted to be spied on this way, so
airplanes were sent to shoot down
enemy observation balloons. A

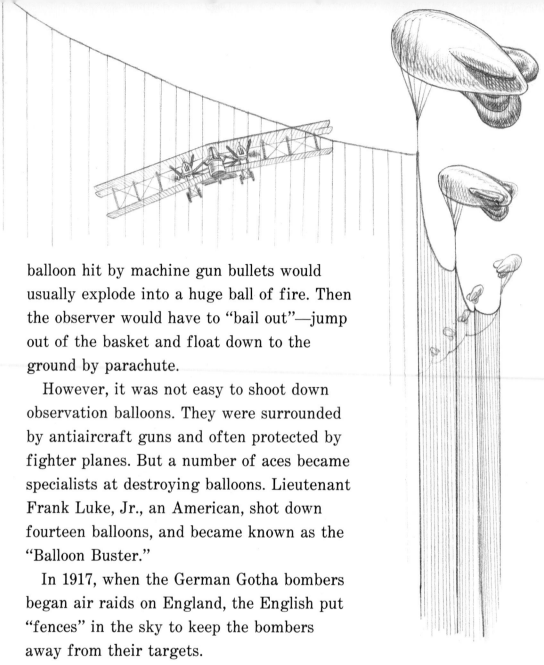

balloon hit by machine gun bullets would usually explode into a huge ball of fire. Then the observer would have to "bail out"—jump out of the basket and float down to the ground by parachute.

However, it was not easy to shoot down observation balloons. They were surrounded by antiaircraft guns and often protected by fighter planes. But a number of aces became specialists at destroying balloons. Lieutenant Frank Luke, Jr., an American, shot down fourteen balloons, and became known as the "Balloon Buster."

In 1917, when the German Gotha bombers began air raids on England, the English put "fences" in the sky to keep the bombers away from their targets.

These fences were formed by groups of balloons fastened together with a long steel cable. From this cable hung a row of cables, each as much as a thousand feet (300 meters) long. Any plane flying into these dangling cables would be smashed up and go hurtling to the ground. All German pilots feared these sky fences.

Famous Flights
and Flights of Fancy

Barnstormers

When World War I ended, armies let most of their airplane pilots go. With no war to fight, they did not need as many fliers.

Many of these men wanted to keep on flying. But there were no jobs for fliers then. There were no airlines yet, and most people thought airplanes would never be of much use, except during a war.

However, some pilots figured out how to make a living by flying. The United States Army decided to get rid of many of its airplanes, as well as its fliers, so some pilots were able to buy an airplane cheap. With these planes, the fliers became entertainers.

After World War I, many pilots earned a living by barnstorming—doing stunt flying and selling flights. This barnstormer raced against a racing car to entertain at a fair.

Barnstormers often did dangerous stunts such as standing on wings or going from one flying airplane to another!

In those days, there was always a fair, carnival, or circus going on in a small town somewhere. Fliers would take their planes to those towns and entertain. For money, they would fight mock air battles against each other and perform flying stunts to thrill the crowds. Many of them did dangerous tricks, such as

standing on a plane's wing or hanging from
its wheel—while it was flying. And they
would sell rides in their airplanes to people
who wanted to find out what it was like to
fly.

These pilots became known as
"barnstormers." They did not know it, but
they were doing something very important.
They were helping to build an interest in
airplanes and flying.

This U.S. Navy flying boat, the *NC-4*, was the first airplane to fly across the Atlantic Ocean.

Famous flying firsts

By the end of World War I, airplanes could fly more than 100 miles (160 kilometers) an hour and stay in the air for a long time. But there were still many things people had not done in an airplane, and a lot of fliers wanted to do new things.

For example, no airplane had flown across an ocean. In 1919, the U.S. Secretary of the Navy decided to see if the Navy's big Curtiss flying boats could do this.

On May 5, 1919, three of the flying boats took off from Newfoundland, Canada, and headed out over the Atlantic Ocean. After eleven hours of flying, two of the planes were in trouble and had to "land" on the water. A ship picked up the crew of one plane. The other simply became a boat and "sailed" into the nearest port.

However, the third plane, the *NC-4*, kept on flying. After fifteen hours, it landed on a small island some 800 miles (1,280 km) off the coast of Europe. It flew on to Portugal the next morning, and so became the first aircraft to cross the Atlantic Ocean. It was flown by a crew of five U.S. Navy men. Of course, the *NC-4* had made that one stop before reaching Europe. Many pilots wanted to fly across the ocean without stopping.

On June 14, 1919, two British airmen, John Alcock and Arthur Brown, took off from Newfoundland in a British Air Force bomber

to try to fly nonstop across the Atlantic Ocean. Flying through the night, they ran into terrible storms. Once, the plane became covered with ice and nearly turned over. But after sixteen hours and twenty-seven minutes of steady flying, the men landed in Ireland. Alcock and Brown were the first to fly across the Atlantic without stopping.

There were still lots of "firsts" to try. On April 6, 1924, four big Douglas World Cruisers, each with a two-man crew, took off from Seattle, Washington, in an attempt to fly around the world. The four planes headed west from Seattle. And 175 days later, two of the planes returned to Seattle coming from the east. They were the first planes to fly around the world. They traveled 27,553 miles (44,298 km) and made 56 stops in 28 countries. (The other two planes were not able to finish the flight.)

When ice formed on their plane's wings, either Alcock or Brown had to crawl out and chip it off!

Several men had tried to reach the North Pole by balloon or airship and had failed. But on May 9, 1926, U.S. Navy Commander Richard E. Byrd and pilot Floyd Bennett flew over it in an airplane. Two days later, the famous Norwegian explorer Roald Amundsen and his party flew over the North Pole in the dirigible *Norge*.

Charles Lindbergh made the first nonstop solo flight across the Atlantic Ocean.

Alcock and Brown had flown across the Atlantic Ocean without stopping, but no one had ever flown alone across an ocean. Then in 1927, a young American pilot, Charles Lindbergh, flew alone, nonstop, from New York to Paris, France. He became known as

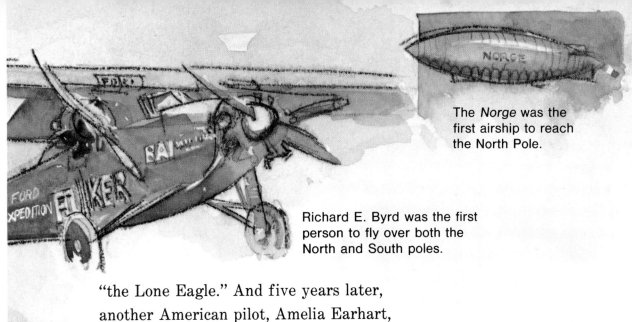

The *Norge* was the first airship to reach the North Pole.

Richard E. Byrd was the first person to fly over both the North and South poles.

"the Lone Eagle." And five years later, another American pilot, Amelia Earhart, became the first woman to fly alone, nonstop, across the Atlantic Ocean.

In 1928, two Americans and two Australians became the first to fly from the United States to Australia. They took off from San Francisco on May 31 and landed in Brisbane, Australia, on June 9, after making stops at Hawaii and the Fiji Islands. Their plane was named *Southern Cross*.

On November 29, 1929, one of the first men to fly over the North Pole also became one of the first to reach the South Pole by air. On that day, Richard E. Byrd, by then a rear admiral, flew over the South Pole with three other men.

The *Southern Cross* was the first airplane to fly from the United States to Australia.

Wiley Post and
the *Winnie Mae*

Landing on a rough field
in Alaska, Wiley Post's
Winnie Mae tipped over.
The round-the-world flight
almost ended right there.
But workers got the plane
upright again.

A crowd cheers Amelia Earhart, who has just landed in
Ireland after flying alone across the Atlantic in 1932.

In 1933, American Wiley Post became the first to fly around the world alone. He did it in seven days, eighteen hours, and forty-nine minutes (with stops, of course), in a plane named *Winnie Mae*.

There were many other "firsts" in the 1920's and 1930's—the first nonstop flight from New York to California, the first flight from England to Australia, and others. Most of these may not seem important now, because they are done easily every day. But remember, even the most common air trip of today was a dangerous, difficult, very special event the first time it was made.

After World War I, British Handley Page bombers like this one were converted to airliners.

The first airliner

During World War I, the Farman Company built many French war planes. In 1918, the company built a big, two-winged, two-engine bomber, the Farman Goliath. But by the time the plane was finished, it was clear that the war was nearly over and there would soon be little need for bombers. The men who ran the Farman company began looking for some other use for the Farman Goliath.

The plane was big enough to hold a number of people. Someone had the idea of using the Goliath to carry passengers long distances—a sort of bus in the sky. Seats were put in and windows were put along the sides of the body so passengers could see out.

And so, the plane that started out as a bomber became the world's first airliner!

The first airline flight took place on February 8, 1919, when the Farman Goliath carried passengers from France to England. At first, there were seats for only twelve people. There was no stereo. There were no movies—none of the things that are on an airliner today. In fact, the inside of the plane wasn't even heated. The passengers had to sit all bundled up in their overcoats!

But as time went on improvements were made and more Goliaths were built. Other companies began building airliners, too. By the middle of the 1920's, airliners were bigger and more comfortable. And some of them even served refreshments during a flight.

The first airliners were not heated. Passengers had to wear overcoats to keep warm.

Dr. Robert Goddard was the first American scientist to dream of sending a rocket into space. This photograph was taken in 1926.

The rocket man

On March 16, 1926, a man had his picture taken standing in a snow-covered field beside a strange-looking metal framework he had built. A short time later, with a roar and a trail of smoke, part of the framework went hurtling into the sky, up and up until it was only a speck. The world's first liquid-fuel rocket had just been launched.

The rocket was built by Dr. Robert H. Goddard, an American scientist. At a time when pilots dreamed of flying farther, faster, or higher than anyone else, Dr. Goddard dreamed of building a rocket that could carry scientific instruments high into the upper part of the atmosphere, where planes and balloons couldn't go. He kept building better rockets through the 1920's and 1930's. In 1935, he sent a rocket almost 4,800 feet (1,440 meters) into the sky.

Many people laughed at Goddard when he began working with rockets in 1912. He was often called "the moon man," because he once said he thought it might be possible to send a rocket all the way to the moon. Most people thought this couldn't be done. But today, Robert Goddard is honored as one of the men who made space flight possible. His work with rockets, rocket engines, and rocket fuels helped others to build spacecraft that did go to the moon.

The man who built a spaceship

A man named Hermann Oberth built a spaceship in 1929. It wasn't a real spaceship, of course, just a pretend spaceship that was built for a German science-fiction movie, *The Lady on the Moon*. However, it was built with all the things a spaceship needs. With the right kind of engine, it might have been able to go into space.

Hermann Oberth was an Austrian schoolteacher. As a young man, he became very interested in the idea of going into space, and he worked out plans for building a spaceship. In 1923, he wrote a book about space flight that got many other people interested in spaceships. He became so famous that a German movie company asked him to build a spaceship for the movie.

Like Konstantin Tsiolkovsky of Russia and Robert Goddard of the United States, Hermann Oberth was one of the men who helped make space flight possible. Many of his plans and ideas for spaceships were used later, when people began building real spaceships.

This scene from a 1929 German science-fiction movie
shows a model of the rocket ship designed by Hermann Oberth.

Exploring the stratosphere

The airplanes flying at the beginning of the 1930's were not much like the planes of today. Most airplanes in the 1930's still had open cockpits in which the pilot sat with his or her head and shoulders out in the air. Some had closed cabins, but the cabins were not heated and they were not *pressurized*, or sealed up tight so that air could not leak out.

Because of this, no airplane at that time could go much higher than about six miles (10 kilometers). Beyond that, the plane would

Dr. Auguste Piccard (right) and an assistant, Paul Kipfer, wearing the special helmets they made to protect their heads on what was to become a record-breaking trip into the stratosphere.

be approaching the stratosphere—the higher part of earth's air, where it is terribly cold, the air is too thin to breathe, and there is much less air pressure. To fly a plane into the stratosphere at that time would have meant certain death.

However, some people had good reasons for wanting to get up into the stratosphere. One was Swiss physicist Auguste Piccard. He wanted to find out about certain rays that come into earth's atmosphere from outer space, and the best place to study them was in the stratosphere. Dr. Piccard knew there was no way he could go up as high as he needed to in an airplane—but he thought he might be able to do it in a balloon.

Of course, he couldn't stay alive if he rode into the stratosphere in the kind of open basket that usually hung beneath a balloon. So he invented a new kind of basket—a round, hollow ball made of aluminum. It contained machinery for making air and it was sealed tight so the air would not leak out. It also contained machinery for recording and measuring the rays that Dr. Piccard was studying.

Piccard had a very large, strong balloon made and the hollow ball was attached beneath it. On May 27, 1931, he and an assistant, Paul Kipfer, entered the ball and took off for the stratosphere. In just half an hour, they reached an altitude of nearly ten

miles (about 16 kilometers). This was the
highest any human had ever gone up to then.

In the years after that, many other people
went much higher. But Auguste Piccard and
Paul Kipfer were the first persons to explore
the stratosphere—and they got there by
balloon.

The *Graf Zeppelin*

In the 1930's, one of the most famous of all aircraft was the *Graf Zeppelin*. The *Graf Zeppelin* was a rigid airship, built in Germany and named for the man who had built the first rigid airship, Graf (Count) von Zeppelin. It was more than 770 feet (235 meters) long, and it was a thrilling sight for people of those days—especially children—to see that huge, silvery shape floating in the sky.

The *Graf Zeppelin* became famous as the

An airport crew helps bring the *Graf Zeppelin* down to a landing in 1929.

The cabin of a zeppelin
was roomy and comfortable.
At one time, many people
thought a zeppelin would
always be the best way to
travel by air.

first airship to fly around the world. On
August 15, 1929, it flew east from Germany
and crossed Russia to Tokyo, Japan. From
there it crossed the Pacific Ocean to Los
Angeles, then flew east across the United
States to Lakehurst, New Jersey. It then
crossed the Atlantic Ocean on its return to
Germany.

The *Graf Zeppelin* made many other long
trips during the 1930's, carrying passengers
over the Atlantic Ocean from Europe to
North and South America and back. At that
time, the only way to cross an ocean by air
was on the *Graf Zeppelin* or another airship.
Most people thought this would always be the
best means of air travel.

Disaster!

Zeppelins that carried passengers back and forth between Europe and North and South America were once fairly common. Today, there are no airships carrying passengers. Airship travel stopped after a terrible disaster that took place almost half a century ago.

On May 4, 1937, the zeppelin *Hindenburg* took off from Germany. The *Hindenburg* was the world's largest airship, more than 800 feet (244 meters) long. It carried a crew of sixty-one and thirty-six passengers. It could also carry more than thirteen tons (11.8 metric tons) of freight.

The *Hindenburg* sped over Europe and headed out across the Atlantic Ocean. Two days later, at nine-thirty on the night of May 6, the huge gray airship reached its landing place at Lakehurst, New Jersey. It began to come down toward the tower to which it would be fastened. A small crowd of newspaper reporters was on hand to watch the landing, for this was only the *Hindenburg*'s second trip to the United States.

Suddenly, the rear end of the *Hindenburg* burst into a sheet of flame! In seconds, the entire airship was afire. The *Hindenburg* sank to the ground, blazing from end to end!

Amazingly, only thirty-six of the

This photograph shows the zeppelin *Hindenburg* burning and falling to the ground in the terrible disaster that killed ninety-seven people.

ninety-seven people on the *Hindenburg* were killed. The rest managed to escape, although many were badly burned.

To this day, no one knows what caused the *Hindenburg* to catch fire. But it burned so swiftly and terribly because it was filled with hydrogen gas, which catches fire very easily. Today's airships, such as the Goodyear blimps, are filled with helium gas, which cannot catch fire.

However, the destruction of the *Hindenburg* meant the end for passenger zeppelins. Everyone felt they were too unsafe. No zeppelin ever carried passengers again and no more zeppelins were ever built. Today, they no longer exist.

The first jet airplane flight

For thirty-six years after the Wright brothers' first flight at Kitty Hawk, every airplane had a propeller. Some had two, three, or even four propellers. Attached to an engine that made it turn, the spinning propeller pulled or pushed the airplane through the air.

But in 1939, the Germans built an airplane that could fly without a propeller. It had a different kind of engine—a jet engine.

An ordinary engine uses the power of exploding gasoline to make parts of the engine move, such as the spinning shaft that turns the propeller. But a jet engine uses

burning fuel to make the whole engine move
forward. As the fuel burns, hot gas shoots
out the back of the engine, and this thrusts
the engine forward. If the engine is mounted
on an airplane, it carries the plane along with
it. A plane with a jet engine can fly much
faster than a plane with a propeller.

The Heinkel Company in Germany built
the first plane to fly with what is now called
a turbojet engine. Called the He 178, this
aircraft was built as a warplane, and the
man who first flew it on August 24, 1939,
was an officer of the German air force.

Ten days later, World War II began. But
most of the planes that would fight in that
war would still be propeller planes.

Wings and Rockets in World War II

Japanese Zero fighter

Warplanes of World War II

World War II began in September 1939. Nearly six years later, the most terrible war in history finally ended in September 1945. More than fifty nations took part in the war. On one side were the Allies, including the United States, Great Britain, France, Russia, Canada, and Australia. On the other side, known as the Axis, the

British Supermarine Spitfires

Italian Macchi MC 200 fighter

German Ju.87 Stuka
dive bomber

three chief nations were
Germany, Italy, and Japan.

At the beginning of the war, all
the main nations had hundreds of
warplanes. These planes could fly
more than two hundred or even
three hundred miles (320-480
kilometers) per hour. They
generally had three or four
machine guns, and some had one
or two small cannons.

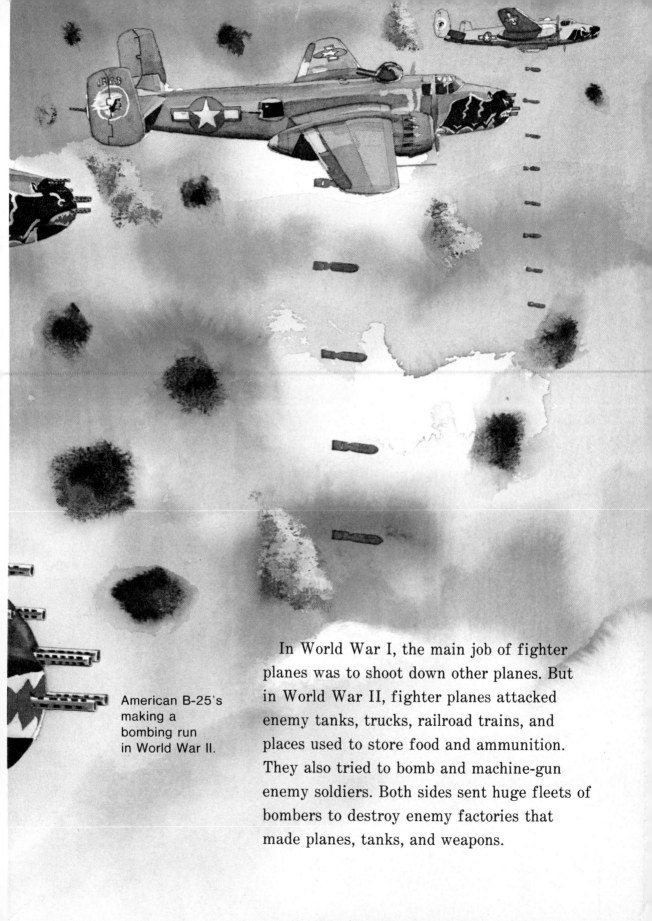

American B-25's
making a
bombing run
in World War II.

In World War I, the main job of fighter planes was to shoot down other planes. But in World War II, fighter planes attacked enemy tanks, trucks, railroad trains, and places used to store food and ammunition. They also tried to bomb and machine-gun enemy soldiers. Both sides sent huge fleets of bombers to destroy enemy factories that made planes, tanks, and weapons.

The biggest sea battles of World War II took place between airplanes and ships. These Japanese torpedo-bombers are attacking an American aircraft carrier.

Navies also used airplanes a great deal to try to bomb and destroy enemy ships. The biggest sea battles of World War II were fought by planes against ships. Most navies had huge aircraft carriers. These floating airfields could carry dozens and dozens of planes.

This picture, taken during World War II, shows U.S. Navy
fighters, torpedo-bombers, and dive bombers sitting with
folded wings on the flight deck of an American carrier.

The Battle of Britain

A huge flight of sixty airplanes droned through the gray, clouded skies above the strip of sea between England and France. The planes' wings and sides bore black crosses outlined in white, the symbol of the German air force. Some of the planes were bombers, bringing loads of destruction to rain down on English factories, harbors, shipyards, and airfields. Others were fighter planes, whose job was to protect the bombers.

But the British knew that the enemy was coming. Almost from the moment the

Germans had left their air bases in France,
they had been tracked by radar. Now, as the
planes crossed over the white cliffs that line
the edge of England, men watched them
through field glasses, counting them and
making sure which way they were headed.
Quickly, the men began to make phone calls.

In places that got the calls, antiaircraft
gun crews got ready. When the planes
appeared, black puffs of smoke began to
burst around them. The antiaircraft guns
hurled up shells that exploded in the sky and
sent chunks of metal whizzing through the
air. As the planes pushed on, some of the

shells hit them. A bomber went screaming down to earth, spinning around and around with a thick plume of black smoke trailing from its tail. A fighter took a direct hit and came apart in midair.

Now, dozens of planes came swarming up from below. They bore blue, white, and red circles—symbols of the British Royal Air Force. Fiery flashes of light winked at the edges of their wings, and the air was filled with a chattering sound as they opened fire with their machine guns. These were British fighter planes, coming up to knock down as many German bombers as they could.

London firemen fighting fires started by German bombs dropped in an air raid during the Battle of Britain.

German fighters dived down to meet the British planes, their wings also flashing with machine-gun fire as they tried to keep the British planes from reaching the bombers. Planes of both sides burst into flame, or blew apart, or went twisting down out of the sky.

Some of the bombers were shot down, but many reached their target and dropped their bombs. Explosions shook the ground and buildings blew apart. Clouds of smoke rolled into the sky.

Huge air battles such as this took place over England several times every day and night from July 10 to October 31, 1940. That long period of daily air raids and air fights is known as the Battle of Britain. During those days Germany sent thousands of planes to England, not only to drop bombs but also to shoot down as many British planes as possible. The Germans felt that if they could wipe out the British air force, they could invade England and win the war.

But the British pilots shot down as many German planes as they could. By October 31, the British had lost 915 planes, but the Germans had lost far more—1,733. Germany eventually had to give up its plan to invade England. The British pilots had saved their nation.

Winston Churchill, the British prime minister, summed up their courageous deeds in these words, "Never . . . was so much owed by so many to so few."

Submarine hunters

In World War II, airships weren't used as
bombers as they had been in World War I.
But the U.S. Navy used them in a different
way—to hunt for enemy submarines. German
submarines would lie in wait near the
American coast and attack ships that sailed
out with supplies meant for soldiers fighting
in Europe and Africa. It was the job of the
airships to find the submarines before they
could attack.

From the sky, a submarine moving near
the surface of the water looked like a long,
dark shadow. Airplanes moved so fast they
might pass right over such a shadow without
seeing it. But the airships moved much more

An American blimp
landing on the deck of
an aircraft carrier
during World War II.
Blimps were used as
submarine hunters.

slowly, and their crews had plenty of time to
study the water beneath them. An airship
was ideal for hunting submarines.

During World War II, the U.S. Navy had
about 135 airships that hunted submarines.
These rather short, squat airships were
known as "blimps."

When a blimp sighted a submarine it would
quickly radio a message to nearby destroyers—
ships whose main job was to attack submarines.
The destroyers would hurry to the spot and
drop depth charges—bombs that exploded
underwater. If a depth charge exploded near a
submarine, it could damage the sub or sink it.

One blimp tried to fight a submarine all by
itself. In 1943, Blimp K-74 found a German
submarine that had surfaced off the coast of
Florida. The blimp attacked, its crew firing
machine guns at the submarine. But the
submarine fired back and shot so many bullet
holes in the blimp that gas began to leak out
and it drifted down into the water. The
submarine escaped, but was sunk some time
later. All but one of the airship's crew was
rescued. The blimp lost that battle, but German
submarines still feared these hunter airships.

Flying bombs!

On a flat stretch of land in Holland stood a towering metal shape. It looked like a giant bomb in a maze of scaffolding. Inside a nearby building, a man reached out and flicked a switch. Clouds of smoke began to pour out of the giant bomb's tail. A steady, thundering roar filled the air.

Abruptly, the smoke became a jet of roaring flame. Slowly, slowly, the huge metal object began to rise off the ground. For a moment it seemed to hang motionless, as if it were balanced on the flame spurting out of its tail. Then it rose faster and faster. High in the air, it tilted slightly, still soaring up in a rising curve until it was out of sight.

Steadily, the flying bomb's speed increased. Now it was moving at more than 3,300 miles (5,300 kilometers) per hour. It was high in the sky—almost at the very edge of space.

Then it began to curve downward. It slanted down across France and then the English Channel. Lower and lower it dropped, until at last it struck the ground in England and blew up with an ear-shattering roar.

This giant flying bomb was a German secret weapon of World War II, known as the V-2, or Vengeance Weapon. Thousands of V-2 guided missiles were fired at England and parts of France and Belgium during the last months of the war. Because the V-2 traveled faster than the speed of sound, people in target cities could not hear it coming. The V-2 did a great deal of damage and killed more than 2,800 people.

But the V-2 was more than just a weapon. It was a model spaceship. The men who built the V-2's had followed the ideas of Konstantin Tsiolkovsky, Robert Goddard, and Hermann Oberth. They had made a rocket engine that was almost powerful enough to carry a huge, heavy object such as a flying bomb out into space.

When World War II ended, the United States and Russia captured the unused V-2's, as well as the scientists who had worked on them. These men helped American and Russian scientists develop the V-2's into the first true spacecraft.

Faster,
Farther,
Higher

Breaking the sound barrier

Near the end of World War II, some propeller planes could fly more than 400 miles (640 kilometers) per hour. But German airplane builders made a fighter plane with a jet engine that could fly nearly 550 miles (885 km) per hour. They also built a plane with a rocket engine, the engine used on V-2's, that could fly more than 600 miles (960 km) per hour.

Many fliers and scientists did not think an airplane could ever go much faster than that. If a plane went much faster, it would be

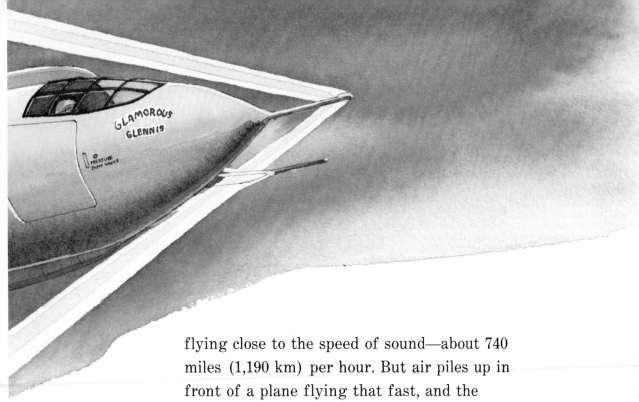

flying close to the speed of sound—about 740 miles (1,190 km) per hour. But air piles up in front of a plane flying that fast, and the effort to push through the air could make the plane shake itself to pieces. It seemed as if the speed of sound was a barrier that could not be broken.

But in the United States, shortly after the end of the war, the Bell Aircraft Company built a plane shaped like a bullet. (A bullet travels many times faster than the speed of sound.) The wings and tail had thin front edges to help them slice through piled-up air. And a powerful rocket engine would thrust the plane through piled-up air. This new plane was called the XS-1, which stood for "Experimental Supersonic One." *Supersonic* means "beyond sound." This plane, later called just X-1, was going to try to break the sound barrier.

On October 14, 1947, a Superfortress bomber carried the X-1 and its pilot, Air

Force Captain Charles Yeager, high into the sky. At an altitude of thirty thousand feet (9,000 meters), the X-1 was dropped from the Superfortress and Captain Yeager turned on its engine.

Soon, Yeager and the X-1 were racing through the sky at 600 miles (965 km) per hour, then 700 miles (1,126 km) per hour. Finally, with only a little shaking, the X-1 reached a speed of 760 miles (1,216 km) per hour—faster than the speed of sound. Yeager had broken the sound barrier.

Today, many warplanes and some jet airliners can fly two, even three, times faster than sound. And special planes have been built and tested that can fly as much as five times the speed of sound.

Captain Charles Yeager in the cockpit of the X-1, in which he became the first person to fly faster than the speed of sound.

Higher and higher

For ten years after World War II, scientists in the United States and the Soviet Union tested rockets. They began with captured German V-2 rockets, but within a few years they were building rockets that were far better than V-2's. As time went on, the rockets went higher and higher.

In 1949, the United States tested the first of its Viking rockets. Viking 1 went up 50 miles (80 kilometers). A year later, Viking 4 went more than twice as high, 105 miles (168 km). In 1951, another Viking made it to 136 miles (217 km). And in 1952, still another Viking reached 158 miles (252 km).

Both the United States and the Soviet Union intended to launch a rocket that would go into orbit. It would circle around and around the world like an artificial moon. With every rocket sent up, they learned more and brought that day closer.

A U.S. Viking rocket goes roaring up toward the stratosphere in a launching in 1955.

The *Lucky Lady II* (lower airplane) had to be refueled in the air several times during its nonstop flight around the world.

Around the world without a stop

For several days the crew of the U.S. B-50 bomber *Lucky Lady II* had known they were going on a secret mission. There was no war, so the mission certainly wasn't a bombing attack. The men wondered what it could be.

Two days before the mission began, they were told what they were going to do. They were to be the first men to fly around the world without stopping.

Early on the morning of February 26, 1949, the big four-engine plane took off from Carswell Air Force Base in Texas. It headed

east across the United States and out over
the Atlantic Ocean. Near the coast of Africa,
two tanker planes met the big bomber. One
at a time, they let long hoses down to *Lucky
Lady II*'s fuel tanks and refueled the plane
in the sky.

Lucky Lady II was refueled in the air
again over Saudi Arabia and the Philippines,
and, finally, over Johnston Island in the
middle of the Pacific Ocean. It came roaring
in to land at Carswell Base at about 9:30 A.M.
on March 2. It had covered 23,452 miles
(37,700 km) in 94 hours—a little less than
four full days—without landing. This was the
first nonstop flight around the world.

U.S. F-86 Sabre

Jets and whirlybirds of war

High above the rolling brown hills of North Korea, hundreds of jet airplanes dived, turned, twisted, and climbed at speeds of more than six hundred miles (965 km) per hour, trying to shoot each other down. The Korean War was on—the first war in which jet airplanes fought against each other.

The war lasted from June 25, 1950, until July 27, 1953. In it, North Korea and China fought South Korea and sixteen United Nations countries, including the United States, Great Britain, Canada, Australia, and New Zealand.

The two main fighter planes used in the Korean War were the American F-86 Sabre jet and the Russian MiG-15 jet fighter. But propeller planes were also used. Huge, four-engine Boeing B-29 Superfortress bombers blasted targets in North Korea. Big twin-engine cargo planes dropped supplies by parachute to men on the ground.

The Korean War was also the first war in which helicopters, or "whirlybirds," were used. Helicopters carried soldiers into places that could not be reached on foot or in trucks or jeeps. They were also used to rescue pilots shot down in the ocean and to whisk wounded soldiers from the battlefield to a hospital.

Russian MiG-15

An artificial moon!

On October 4, 1957, a huge rocket went thundering up from a plain in Russia. Its powerful engine drove it at a speed of nearly five miles (8 km) per second. The rocket quickly reached an altitude of 142 miles (228 km) in the blackness of space.

Then the rocket's pointed, hollow nose automatically pushed off, and a metal globe about the size of a basketball was hurled into space. The globe was moving just fast enough to go into orbit, moving around and around the Earth.

Four long, slim antennae automatically opened up out of the metal ball and began working. Scientists listening to a special radio station on earth began hearing a steady high *beep—beep—beep*. It was a signal that the globe was out in space, moving around Earth—a tiny artificial moon.

The successful launching of the first artificial satellite into space created tremendous excitement. The metal globe became known as *Sputnik*, which means "traveler" in Russian.

Sputnik stayed in orbit around Earth for 94 days. It made one full circle every 96 minutes. It sent radio signals back carrying information on such things as its temperature and the conditions in space around it.

As *Sputnik* orbited the Earth, gravity
tugged at it steadily, pulling it lower. At last,
it sank down into the atmosphere—the
"wrapper" of air around the Earth. There,
friction, the rubbing together of air and the
metal globe, made the globe hotter and
hotter until it finally burned up.

Sputnik was humanity's first real step into
space. The conquest of space had begun.

Into Space

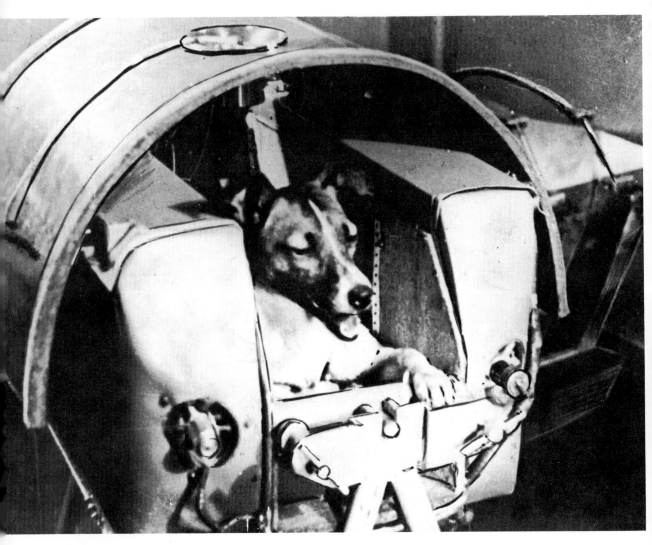

The dog named Laika was the first living creature from Earth to go into orbit in space.

The first earth creature in space

Now that an object from Earth had been launched into space, almost everyone felt it wouldn't be long before a human would go into space. But, just as animals had been used to make sure it was safe for humans to go up in a balloon, Russian scientists now used an animal to make sure that space flight would be safe for humans. On November 3, 1957, a female dog named Laika became the first earth creature to travel in space.

Laika rode into space in a cone-shaped spacecraft that was tucked inside the hollow nose of a huge rocket. When the rocket got out into space, the nose cone dropped off and Laika's spacecraft, *Sputnik II*, shot out into orbit around the Earth.

Laika was specially trained for her great journey so that she wouldn't be frightened by the terrible noise and shaking when the rocket took off. Her spacecraft was thickly padded, heated, and air-conditioned to keep her as comfortable as possible. Special machinery automatically fed her meals several times a day.

Other machinery in the spacecraft kept check on Laika's heart, how fast she was breathing, and other things. The machinery showed that Laika stayed normal and healthy during her seven days in space. Thus, scientists knew that space travel would be safe for humans.

Sadly, there was no way to get Laika back to Earth. And so, one of her meals contained a quick-acting, painless drug. Laika went to sleep and never woke up again. She was a heroine whose name will never be forgotten!

A photograph of a nearly full moon taken from the *Apollo 8* spacecraft.

Reaching for the moon

The moon is the closest object in space to Earth, and people have always wondered about it. Long ago, many people worshiped it as a god or goddess. Later, people realized it was a planet, with mountain ranges and broad plains. They wondered if it had air and water, and if there could be living things on it. They also wondered what its other side looked like, because the moon has always shown only one side to the Earth. Many people dreamed of somehow reaching the moon and finding out about all these things.

A little more than a year after Laika went into space, the dream of reaching the moon began to come true. Now that scientists could send things out into space, they planned to send special spacecraft to the moon—craft that could tell them the things they wanted to know.

The first craft to be sent to the moon was named *Luna*, after the moon's scientific name. Russian scientists launched *Luna*, a round metal ball with four slim antennae, in the nose of a rocket on January 2, 1959.

Unlike *Sputnik I* and *Sputnik II*, *Luna* was moving fast enough to escape from Earth's gravity. Instead of going into orbit around earth, it sped on into space. It missed the moon by about 3,500 miles (5,630 kilometers), and went into orbit around the sun. But as it passed the moon, machinery inside it sent important information back to Earth about what space near the moon is like.

This information helped when Russian scientists launched *Luna 2* on September 12, 1959. They wanted *Luna 2* to actually *hit* the moon. That isn't as easy as it might sound. The moon is always moving, so *Luna 2* had to be sent at a speed that would get it to where the moon was going to be by the time *Luna 2* reached the moon's orbit path. But everything worked out right, and *Luna 2* came down on the moon.

Luna 2 was the first thing ever sent from Earth to another object in space. It smashed up when it hit the moon. But first, its

machinery sent important information to Earth.

The next moon visitor, *Luna 3*, was a more complicated machine with a special purpose. Scientists had worked out *Luna 3*'s flight so that it would go around the moon, passing by the far side.

Luna 3, launched on October 4, 1959, went around the moon, just as it was supposed to do. And it took photographs of the moon's far side and sent them back to Earth by television. At last, after thousands of years of wondering, people finally learned what the moon's far side looks like.

Thus we learned more about the moon in just one year, 1959, than we had in thousands of years.

Luna 3 passing over the moon

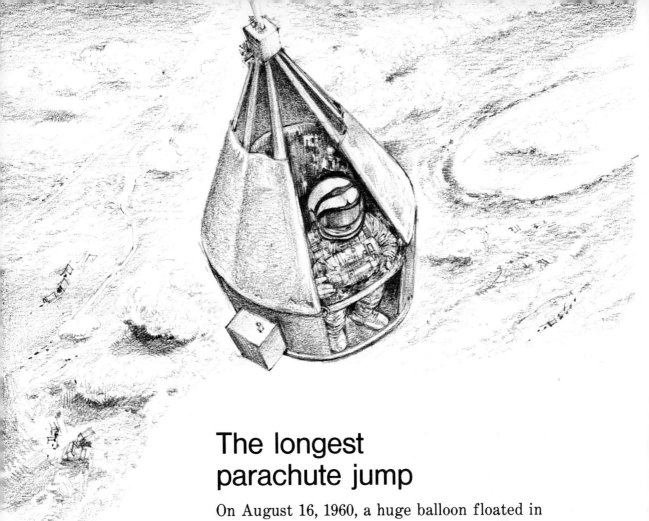

The longest parachute jump

On August 16, 1960, a huge balloon floated in the stratosphere more than nineteen miles (30.4 kilometers) above North America. At that height, there is hardly any air or air pressure, and it is bitterly cold! Even so, a man stood in the open gondola that hung beneath the balloon.

The man, Captain Joseph Kittinger of the United States Air Force, wore a bulky pressure suit that kept him warm and protected him against injury that the low air pressure could cause. A helmet with a glass front covered his head, and containers of oxygen, strapped to his body, kept the helmet filled with air. He also wore a parachute.

Suddenly, Captain Kittinger stepped out of the gondola and began to fall toward the earth, nineteen miles below. By the time he had fallen three miles (4.8 kilometers), he was traveling 615 miles (900 km) per hour, or faster than many jet airplanes fly.

After about four and one-half minutes, the parachute automatically opened and Captain Kittinger floated the rest of the way to the earth. After stepping out of the gondola, he fell through the air for thirteen minutes and forty-five seconds. It was the longest parachute jump in history.

But Captain Kittinger made his parachute jump for better reasons than just to set a record. The United States was getting ready to send men into space, and his jump was made to learn some things that would help the spacemen.

By going up into the stratosphere where it is nearly as cold and airless as space, Captain Kittinger showed that the kind of pressure suits that space explorers would later wear would protect them. His jump also proved that people could survive if they had to parachute from their spacecraft when it was returning to earth.

The first voyagers into space were brave, indeed. But so were those who, like Captain Kittinger, helped find out what needed to be known before anyone could go into space.

19 miles

In 1960, Captain Joseph Kittinger made the world's longest parachute jump. He dropped nineteen miles (30.4 km) and was in the air nearly fourteen minutes.

The space sailor

A rocket sent roaring up out of Russia on
April 12, 1961, was the most important craft
yet fired into space. Far up at the edge of
space, its hollow nose came off, leaving a
small spacecraft, a cylinder with a ball at the
end. A burst of energy from a rocket engine
in the cylinder sent this craft shooting on out
into space in an orbit around the Earth. Then
the cylinder fell away, leaving a round, metal
ball attached to a broad, squat cone.

Inside the cone was a small rocket engine.
And inside the ball was a man. This man was

Yuri Gagarin, a major in the Russian Air
Force. He was the first person to go into
space. The Russians called him a *cosmonaut*,
or "space sailor."

In space, the darkness is bitter cold,
sunlight is burning hot, and there is no air.
Yuri Gagarin wore a special space suit and
helmet that protected him from the cold and
heat. Air from tanks on his back was pumped
into his sealed helmet. Of course, there was
air, heat, and air-conditioning inside the
round ball that was Gagarin's craft. But if
the machinery supplying these failed,
Gagarin's space suit would keep him alive.

As the rocket carrying the spacecraft soared up from Earth, Yuri Gagarin lay on a thickly padded couch. The terrible pressure created as the rocket strained to break free of Earth's gravity crushed the cosmonaut down against the padding. But when he got out into space, beyond Earth's gravity, Gagarin found himself floating above the couch. In space, his body was weightless.

The spacecraft made one complete orbit, or circle, of the Earth in about one hour and twenty-nine minutes. At the end of that time, the spacecraft was back over Russia, where it had started.

Now Yuri Gagarin fired the rocket engine. This slowed the speed of his craft and pointed it back toward Earth. Moments later, the metal ball separated from the cone that contained the engine. The ball began to fall to Earth at a speed of almost three hundred feet (90 meters) per second. Only a special shell around the ball kept it from burning up from the sizzling friction.

About two and one-half miles (4 kilometers) above the ground, a huge parachute opened up from the top of the metal ball which then floated gently to earth. Space had truly been conquered. A human being had gone into space and returned safely.

The first space people

Twenty-three days after Yuri Gagarin made his historic flight, an American, Alan B. Shepard, Jr., became the second person to go into space. On May 5, 1961, he made a fifteen-minute test flight into space in a craft named *Freedom 7*.

Another American, Virgil Grissom, became the third spaceman on July 21, 1961. He made a sixteen-minute test flight in a spacecraft named *Liberty Bell*.

On August 6-7, Gherman S. Titov of Russia made sixteen orbits

Alan Shepard, Jr.

Virgil Grissom

in a craft named *Vostok* (East) *2*. He was in space for one full day, one hour, and eighteen minutes.

On February 20, 1962, John H. Glenn, Jr., became the first American to orbit the Earth. He made three orbits in four hours and fifty-five minutes in *Friendship 7*. Just about two months later, Scott Carpenter of the United States also made three orbits, in *Aurora 7*. It took him one minute longer than it had taken Glenn.

Russia sent up two spacecraft, one after the other, on August 11

John Glenn

Scott Carpenter

and 12, 1962. In the first of these, *Vostok 3*, cosmonaut Andrian G. Nikolayev made sixty orbits in three days, twenty-two hours and twenty-two minutes. Cosmonaut Pavel R. Popovich made forty-five orbits in *Vostok 4* in a little less than three days.

American astronaut ("star sailor") Walter M. Schirra, Jr., made the last space voyage of 1962. On October 3, he made six orbits in a little more than nine hours in *Sigma 7*.

On May 16, 1963, American astronaut L. Gordon Cooper, Jr.,

Walter M. Schirra, Jr.

Pavel R. Popovich

Valentina Tereshkova,
first woman in space

went into space for twenty-two orbits. On
June 14, Russian cosmonaut Valery Bykovsky
began a nearly five-day voyage of
seventy-six orbits. And on June 16, the first
woman to go into space, Russian cosmonaut
Valentina Tereshkova, began forty-five orbits
that took a little less than three days.

Thus, by the middle of 1963, a dozen people
had gone into space and returned safely. The
Space Age was well underway.

Taking a "walk" in space

By the beginning of 1965, more than a dozen people had gone into space. Scientists now knew that inside a spacecraft people could eat, sleep, and work in space just as well as they could on earth.

But what if something went wrong with a spacecraft while it was in space? What if some astronauts or cosmonauts had to go outside to fix their ship? What if the crew had to leave their ship and make their way to a rescue ship? They could not fall to earth, of course, for they would simply float. But would floating in space, hundreds of miles above the earth, drive a person crazy?

To find out, scientists decided to see what would happen to a person who tried to "walk" in space.

Russian cosmonaut
Alexei A. Leonov took
the first "spacewalk."

On March 18, Russia sent *Voskhod* (sunrise)
2 into orbit. The craft carried two men—Pavel
I. Belyayev, the pilot, and Alexei A. Leonov,
who was to take the first "spacewalk."

As soon as *Voskhod 2* was in orbit,
cosmonaut Leonov began the experiment. A
thick metal door opened on *Voskhod 2*'s side
and Leonov climbed through it—out into open
space. Fastened to his space suit was a long

cord, or lifeline, that was attached to the ship. He let himself float into the star-filled blackness until the lifeline was stretched tight. He gazed at the gigantic blue, white, and brown ball of Earth below him. Leonov felt as if he were swimming over an enormous map.

This was the moment that many scientists feared would make a person faint or become hysterical. But nothing of that sort happened to Leonov. Instead, he found that floating in space was fun.

The United States launched *Gemini 4* on June 3 with James A. McDivitt as its pilot and Edward H. White as the first American "spacewalker."

Like cosmonaut Leonov, astronaut White had a long lifeline attached to his spacecraft. But Leonov had only been able to float or to pull himself along the line. On the other hand, White could move wherever he wanted to go. He carried a special "gun" that shot squirts of air. Each squirt pushed him in the direction opposite to that in which the gun was pointed. Using this "gun," astronaut White moved himself all around *Gemini 4*.

Astronaut White "walked" in space for twenty-one minutes. And, like cosmonaut Leonov, White found that spacewalking was fun. Leonov and White had shown that space travelers would be able to work outside a ship in space.

U.S. astronaut Edward H. White floats in space,
attached to his spacecraft by a long line.

Far Out
and
Close In

On April 20, 1969, U.S. astronauts Neil Armstrong and Edwin Aldrin (shown here) become the first men to walk on the moon.

A visit to the moon

One of the greatest adventures in history took place on July 20, 1969. A human being stepped onto another world. After a voyage of 240,000 miles (386,000 kilometers) across space, American astronaut Neil Armstrong became the first person to set foot on the moon.

It took nearly eight years of hard work, problem solving, and bitter disappointments before that great moment. For, before anyone could be sent to the moon, we had to learn a lot of things about the moon. And before a "moonship" could even be built, we had to find out many things about space flight.

In the early days of space flight, we knew surprisingly little about the moon. For example, many scientists thought the moon's surface might be covered with a deep layer of dust, and that a spaceship landing there might sink into the dust and be lost. So, the first thing to do was to find out what the moon was really like.

To do this, scientists decided to send "robot explorer" craft to the moon. These robots, called *Rangers*, would land, take pictures, test the soil, and send reports back to earth.

The first Ranger was launched in 1961, but it never got to the moon. It fell back into Earth's atmosphere and burned up. Months of time and millions of dollars were lost. Three months later, when *Ranger 2* was launched—the same thing happened!

The scientists worked to correct the problems, and *Ranger 3* was launched in 1962. It got out into space all right, but it missed the moon by thousands of miles (km).

Bad luck seemed to ride with every Ranger. *Ranger 4* crashed into the moon and didn't send back any information. *Ranger 5* missed the moon and was lost. *Ranger 6* crashed on the moon without sending any information.

But in July 1964, *Ranger 7* was launched. It worked perfectly, sending back many close-up pictures of the moon's surface. *Rangers 8* and *9* also worked perfectly, sending back useful pictures in 1965.

Then, in May 1966, an American *Surveyor* spacecraft landed gently on the moon and sent pictures of the moon's surface. Just two months earlier, a Russian spacecraft, *Luna 9*, had done the same thing. This proved that a spacecraft could land safely on the moon.

Meanwhile, the United States had put eighteen men into space. Each time, more was learned that would make a moon trip safer and easier. In 1965, American astronauts began to practice how to bring two spacecraft together and fasten them to each other in space. This was one of the things men going to the moon would have to be able to do. By 1966, it was all worked out.

A *Surveyor* spacecraft like this one, was the first U.S. spacecraft to land on the moon.

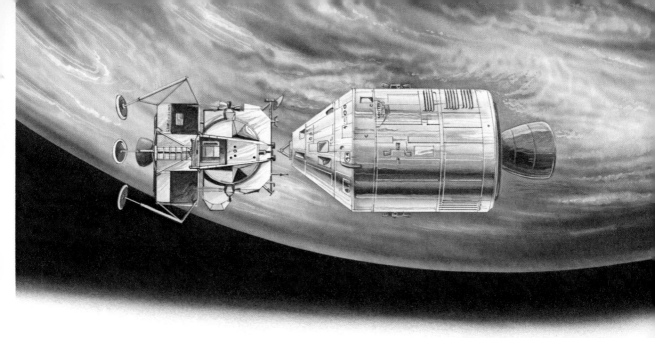

In orbit about Earth, U.S. astronauts practiced docking a LEM with an Apollo to make sure it could be done over the moon.

In 1967, an *Apollo* spacecraft, the kind that would take men to the moon, was sent into space with no one aboard. Controlled from Earth, it was put through all the moves that the actual moonship would have to make, and then brought back. Everything had worked perfectly.

Next, in 1968, came a test of the little craft that would actually land on the moon—the Lunar Excursion Module, or LEM (now simply called a lunar module, or LM). It, too, worked perfectly.

In the six months before the moon landing, a number of special tests were made. To test the spacecraft, three astronauts went to the moon, circled it, and came back. In orbit near the earth, three other astronauts tested the fastening and unfastening of the LEM from the Apollo. Then, a month before the landing, came the last and most important test. Three

"That's one small step for a man, one giant step for mankind," said astronaut Neil Armstrong on Sunday night, July 20, 1969, as he became the first person to set foot on the moon.

astronauts went to the moon and two of them took the LEM down close to the moon's surface, then flew it back up to the Apollo ship again.

On July 16, 1969, *Apollo 11* was launched to the moon. Aboard were Michael Collins, the pilot, and the two astronauts, Edwin Aldrin and Neil Armstrong, who would land the LEM on the moon.

On July 20, *Apollo 11* reached the moon and circled it in orbit. Armstrong and Aldrin entered the LEM and separated it from *Apollo 11*. A blast of the LEM's engine sent it speeding down toward the moon's surface.

There is no air on the moon, so the LEM could not fly down like an airplane. It was actually *falling*, at a speed of more than two miles (3.2 km) a minute. Bursts from the engine slowed it down enough so that it landed gently.

Most of the great moments in the conquest of sky and space, such as the Wright brothers' first flight and Blériot's flight across the English Channel, were not seen by more than a few people. But a television camera mounted on the LEM enabled millions of people to see Neil Armstrong climb out of the LEM and set foot on the moon.

Astronaut Edwin Aldrin put an American flag on the moon.

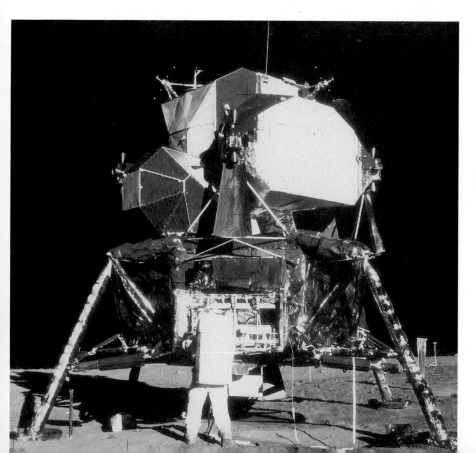

the LEM on the moon

The LEM returning from the surface of the moon to the Apollo command ship. The "half moon" in the background is the Earth.

An astronaut left this footprint on the moon.

Later, Aldrin joined Armstrong. The two men performed experiments with special equipment and dug up samples of moon rocks for scientists to examine. Then they reentered the LEM and flew back to *Apollo 11*. They fastened the LEM to the Apollo and rejoined Collins. Soon, they were on their way home.

Between 1969 and 1972, astronauts made five more trips to the moon. Those were thrilling, exciting events, too. But nothing will ever compare to that day in 1969 when the thing people had dreamed of for thousands of years first came true—and a man from Earth set foot on the moon.

Solving the mystery of Venus

A strange, squat machine sat in the midst of a brown, rocky landscape. In the distance towered a range of enormous mountains. Overhead, flickers of lightning filled a murky, orange sky.

The machine was a visitor from another world. It had come across 185 million miles (298,000,000 kilometers) of space from Earth. Now, it rested on the planet Venus.

After the moon, Venus is the closest heavenly body to Earth. But until the Space Age began, we knew less about Venus than we did about some of the more distant planets. All we really knew was how big it was and that it had some kind of atmosphere.

That atmosphere is what made Venus such a mystery. It is so thick and murky that the surface of Venus cannot be seen. Scientists could not tell if the surface was a great sandy desert or a gigantic ocean. And they could not tell whether the atmosphere was wind-blown dust or oily smog.

Soon after it became possible to send space probes to explore, both the United States and the Soviet Union started trying to learn more about Venus. But the first few space probes, sent in 1960 and 1961, failed.

Then, in August 1962, the United States launched *Mariner* (sailor) *2.* It looked a little

Sun

Mercury

Venus

Earth

Mars

Jupiter

Saturn

Uranus

Neptune

Pluto

Venus is the closest planet to Earth. Both the United States and the Soviet Union have sent space probes to explore it.

like a radio tower standing on a pair of wings, with an automobile steering wheel hanging down one side. It passed within 22,000 miles (35,300 km) of Venus. *Mariner 2* measured the thickness of the atmosphere and also the planet's temperature. Scientists were surprised to learn that Venus is tremendously hot.

In 1965, a Russian craft called *Venera* (Venus) *3* landed on Venus. It was supposed to land gently, so it could send back information, but it crashed.

In 1962, the U.S. *Mariner 2* passed close to Venus and sent back information that the planet is very, very hot.

In 1967, Russian and American space probes reached Venus a day apart. On October 18, the Russian craft, *Venera 4*, floated down through Venus' atmosphere on a parachute. Instruments inside the probe checked, measured, and tested. *Venera 4* sent back the information that the atmosphere of Venus is made up almost entirely of the gas called carbon dioxide, mixed with a tiny bit of oxygen and water vapor.

Russian *Venera* spacecraft on Venus

The American craft, *Mariner 5*, passed Venus on October 19, at a distance of only 2,500 miles (4,000 km), with all its instruments working. One of the things it found out was that Venus has almost no magnetism.

In 1975, a Russian craft landed on Venus and sent back the first pictures ever taken of the surface. The pictures showed the ground strewn with smooth stones and boulders. Later, another craft sent back better pictures that showed a rocky, desertlike landscape.

In 1975, an American craft, *Pioneer Venus 1*, was put into orbit around Venus to take pictures and to map the surface by means of radar. Later that year, *Pioneer Venus 2* shot four small craft into the atmosphere of Venus to do more testing, checking, and measuring. Two more Russian craft also landed on Venus that year, and two more in 1981.

So, we now know quite a lot about Venus. We know that this planet is a huge, rocky desert. In places, there are towering mountains, and some of the mountains are volcanoes. In other places, there are immensely long and deep canyons. The ground is so hot it would make a chunk of lead melt. The sky is orange, and lightning flashes through it. The clouds are formed of sulfuric acid, a liquid that can burn your skin. And winds stronger than hurricanes roar across Venus.

Venus does not seem to be a very nice place for people. But at least, thanks to the Space Age, it's no longer a mystery.

Looking for life on Mars

The planet Mars appears in the night sky as a bright point of reddish light. Because of that, it has long been known as the "Red Planet." For centuries, people have wondered if there might be life on other planets. Many felt that the most likely one to have life was the Red Planet.

There were several reasons for this. In 1877, an Italian astronomer said that while looking at Mars through a telescope, he saw some straight, crisscrossed lines on it. Many people decided these lines must be canals, dug by intelligent creatures.

Another reason was that, through a telescope, Mars looked as if it had plant life. Parts of the planet sometimes grew dark, as

Many people once thought that Mars had canals made by "Martians" to bring water to their cities.

if plants were spreading in summertime. Then, these parts would turn light, as if winter had come and the plants were gone. If there were plants on Mars, there could certainly be animals.

So when the United States and the Soviet Union began to send space probes to Mars, many people were excited. What would the living things on Mars be like, they wondered.

The American spacecraft *Mariner 4* was the first to reach Mars. Launched in November 1964, it passed Mars in July 1965. As it went past, it took pictures that were sent back to Earth by means of television.

Through a telescope, across many millions of miles (kilometers), the surface of Mars is rather blurry. But the pictures showed the surface clearly, from a distance of only about six thousand miles (9,654 km). Scientists were surprised at what the pictures showed. Mars seemed to look like the moon, for it is dotted with craters. No one had even suspected that.

But the *Mariner 4* pictures actually showed only a tiny portion of the surface of Mars. In 1969, *Mariners 6* and *7* took nearly two hundred pictures that showed more of the surface. They also conducted tests and experiments that provided information about the temperature and atmosphere of Mars. And in 1973, *Mariner 9* took more than seven thousand pictures of all parts of the planet.

All this information showed that Mars really isn't much like the moon. The pictures showed a rocky world of mountains, valleys, and canyons, but they showed far fewer craters than are found on the moon. The tests and experiments showed Mars to be a cold place with a thin atmosphere of carbon dioxide gas. Its north and south poles are covered with ice, like the poles on Earth.

Mars does not look like a place where anything could live. None of the pictures showed any canals or any plants. However, some scientists thought there was still a

The American spacecraft *Mariner 9* passing over Mars.

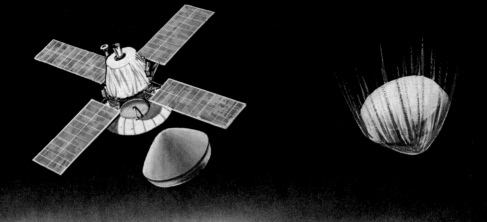

chance there might be some kind of life on Mars—microbes living in the soil. So, the United States built two special *Viking* spacecraft designed to look for that sort of life on Mars.

Each Viking was launched in the nose cone of a big booster rocket. Out in space, after leaving the nose cone, a Viking looked like four big windmill vanes with a large lampshade sticking up in the middle of them on one side, and a big covered bowl hanging down from the other side. The "lampshade" contained instruments and machinery. The vanes collected sunlight and turned it into electricity to run the machinery. And the "bowl" contained a landing craft designed to go down to the surface of Mars.

Launched on August 20, 1975, *Viking 1* reached Mars in June 1976, and went into orbit around the planet. On July 20, a scientist on Earth pressed a button that sent a radio signal through space to start the machinery on the Viking. The "bowl" with

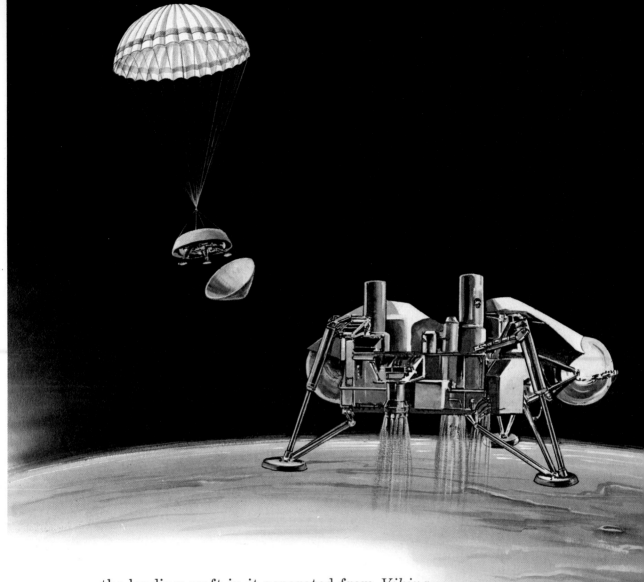

the landing craft in it separated from *Viking 1* and began to drop swiftly toward the surface of Mars.

The bowl was a protective shell that kept the lander from burning up from friction as it fell through the Martian atmosphere. On the way down, a big parachute automatically opened, slowing the lander's fall, and the bowl was automatically cast loose. At the last minute, the lander's rocket engines fired, slowing it down for a gentle landing.

When it was over Mars, the U.S. *Viking 1* released a landing craft inside a protective shield. The shield was cast loose and the lander then drifted down to Mars on a parachute.

The lander was a marvelous machine, a robot laboratory with television cameras on it. First, the camera took a wide picture that showed what Mars would look like to someone standing where the lander was—a reddish-brown desert with rocks scattered all over it, and an orange sky.

On July 28, the laboratory went to work, controlled from Earth by radio signals. It would test to see if there were living things in the soil of Mars!

A metal robot arm reached out and scooped up a bit of soil and brought it into the lander. There it was heated, moistened with a broth, and tested for gas. The broth was food for microbes. If they used it, a gas would form that the lander's instruments could measure.

Viking 1 lander on Mars

A picture of the Martian landscape taken by the *Viking 1* lander.

But the experiment was a disappointment. It showed no evidence of living things in the Martian soil.

Viking 2's lander dropped down onto Mars in September 1976 and also made tests. But these, too, indicated that there probably is no life on Mars. What about the canals? There are no canals. And the darkening that looks like plants spreading out in the summer? Dust storms that fill the sky with sand cause that.

However, the landers and other space probes gave us enough information to show that Mars is a very interesting place, life or no life. It has volcanoes, one of which is three times higher than the highest mountain on Earth. There are long, deep canyons, and one of them is about as long as the United States is wide. Enormous dust storms swirl over the deserts, sometimes lasting for weeks.

Of all the planets we know about, Mars seems to be the one most like the earth. Some time in the future it will probably be visited and explored by people, as the moon was. Perhaps you will be one of the explorers.

Exploring the outer planets

Venus and Mars are millions of miles (kilometers) from Earth. But even so, they are two of Earth's closest neighbors in the solar system. The planets beyond Mars are hundreds of millions, even billions, of miles (km) away. But scientists believed that these planets, too, should be explored.

In 1972, the United States began launching long-distance explorer probes to them. *Pioneer 10*, the first craft launched, looked like a huge silver bowl with a number of poles sticking out of it. It left Earth on March 2, 1972, headed for the planet Jupiter.

Jupiter is the largest planet in the solar system—a giant that is as big as a thousand Earths. We knew quite a bit about Jupiter even before *Pioneer 10* reached it. We knew it was formed mostly of hydrogen gas and had a thick, cloudy atmosphere. We knew it had at least twelve moons, and thought it might even have more.

But there were still many mysteries and puzzles. One of the greatest mysteries was the Red Spot—a reddish blotch in Jupiter's atmosphere. For hundreds of years, scientists had seen it through telescopes. It is three times as big as our world, and it moves around. What could it possibly be? Would *Pioneer 10* be able to tell us?

A photograph of Jupiter, taken from the *Voyager 1* spacecraft.

More than 130 days after leaving Earth, *Pioneer 10* had rushed past Mars and entered the region of space known as the Asteroid Belt. This is an area filled with thousands of big and little rocks called asteroids, all whizzing in orbit around the sun. *Pioneer 10* was the first spacecraft to go into this dangerous region. Could it get through, or would it be struck by a hurtling asteroid and destroyed?

Pioneer 10 got through with no trouble. Then, on December 3, 1973, after a journey of some 390 million miles (624 million km), it reached Jupiter. Passing the huge planet at a distance of about eighty thousand miles (128,000 km), its TV cameras took pictures and its instruments checked, measured, and tested.

When the pictures and information arrived back on Earth, they brought some surprises. Jupiter turned out to be a gigantic ball of mostly liquid hydrogen. Through its cloudy atmosphere rush winds that blow more fiercely than the most terrible tornado or hurricane that ever blew on Earth—winds that move at speeds of as much as three hundred miles (480 km) per hour. The planet gives off great amounts of heat and radiation. As for the Red Spot, that is a kind of giant hurricane that has been swirling in Jupiter's atmosphere for centuries.

Pioneer 10 moved past Jupiter, heading away from the sun. It is the first spacecraft destined to leave the solar system. It will keep going forever!

Jupiter's Red Spot, photographed by *Voyager 1.*

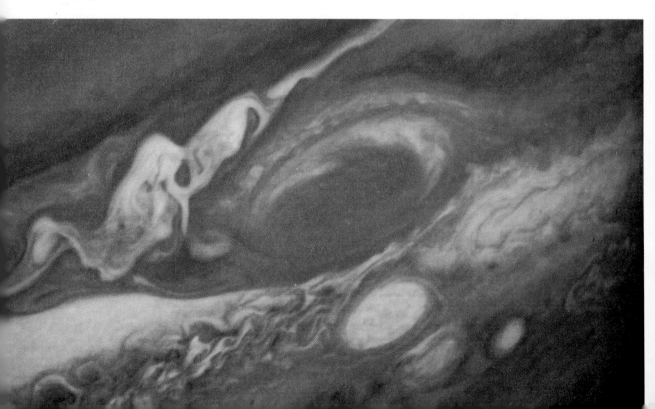

Saturn, photographed by *Voyager 2*.

Even as *Pioneer 10* headed toward Jupiter, *Pioneer 11* left Earth on April 6, 1973. It passed within only twenty-six thousand miles (41,600 km) of Jupiter on December 2, 1974, and sent back more pictures and information.

But unlike *Pioneer 10*, *Pioneer 11*'s work was not finished. Scientists had worked out a slightly different path for it. After passing Jupiter, it headed for Saturn, the second largest planet in the solar system. Saturn is a giant ball of hydrogen and helium gas, surrounded by rings that are formed of millions of chunks of ice. Before *Pioneer 11* reached Saturn, astronomers believed that Saturn had three rings and about nine moons.

The voyage from Jupiter to Saturn took *Pioneer 11* nearly five years. It arrived at

Saturn in November 1980. Once again its camera and instruments went to work, controlled from Earth. The pictures and other information showed that Saturn had one more ring and two more moons than anyone had known about.

By the time *Pioneer 11* reached Saturn, two more spacecraft, *Voyager 1* and *Voyager 2*, had been launched to Jupiter. They resembled the Pioneers in appearance, but were bigger and carried many more instruments to do more things.

Voyager 1 arrived on March 5, 1979, on a path that took it close to some of Jupiter's moons. *Voyager 2* arrived about four months later. Each craft took more than fifteen thousand pictures of Jupiter and its moons.

Scientists learned for the first time that there is a huge ring of rocks and dust encircling Jupiter. The two Voyagers also discovered more moons, bringing the total to sixteen. And we saw the first close-up pictures ever taken of some of Jupiter's main moons—pictures that showed things of which no one on Earth could even have dreamed. Scientists were amazed and delighted when some of the pictures showed that the moon called Io has many live volcanoes that erupt frequently. Until then, everyone thought only Earth had live volcanoes.

Like *Pioneer 11*, both the Voyagers had been launched on paths that would steer

There are live volcanoes on Io, one of Jupiter's sixteen moons. The giant Jupiter, the largest planet in the solar system, fills the sky.

them toward Saturn after they left Jupiter. They went past Jupiter in a way that enabled them to pick up speed from the huge planet's rotation, and this got them to Saturn faster. *Voyager 1* reached Saturn in a little less than two years, *Voyager 2* got there in a little more than two years.

Once again the Voyagers sent back pictures and facts that provided astounding new information. Scientists learned that Saturn actually has seven separate rings, each made up of thousands of thin "ringlets," one inside another. They also discovered that Saturn has twenty-three moons, many more than had been known about. Close-up photos of some of Saturn's moons also provided surprises.

When *Voyager 1* passed Saturn, it headed out of the solar system. But *Voyager 2* headed a different direction. In January 1986, *Voyager 2* will fly past the solar system's seventh planet, Uranus, more than

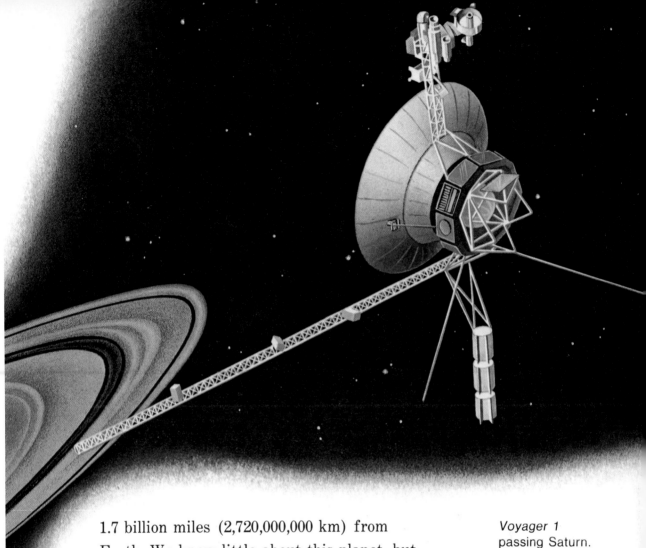

Voyager 1
passing Saturn.

1.7 billion miles (2,720,000,000 km) from
Earth. We know little about this planet, but
if *Voyager 2*'s machinery is still working
when it passes Uranus, we may learn a lot.

After Uranus, *Voyager 2* will head toward
the eighth planet, Neptune, which is about 2.7
billion miles (3,320,000,000 km) from Earth.
Voyager 2 should reach Neptune in 1989.

Then, *Voyager 2* will follow *Voyager 1* and
the two Pioneers out into the endless space
beyond our solar system. Billions of years
from now, unless they should chance to fall
into stars, they will still be traveling through
the vast, star-spangled darkness.

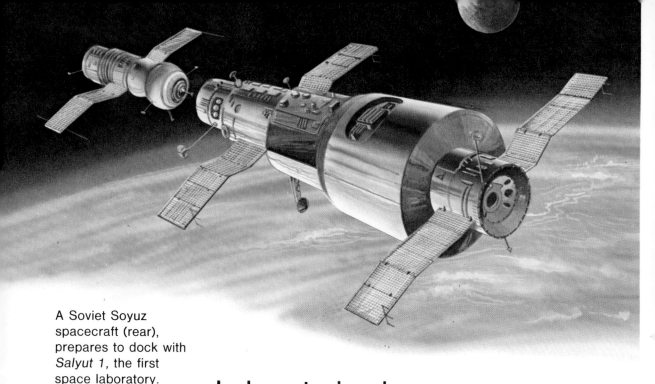

A Soviet Soyuz spacecraft (rear), prepares to dock with *Salyut 1,* the first space laboratory.

Laboratories in space

There are things that can be done in space that can't be done on Earth. Certain materials that won't mix on Earth because of gravity will mix in space. This would make it possible to produce new kinds of metals, medicines, and other useful things in space.

Both the United States and the Soviet Union decided they needed laboratories in space—places where scientists and technicians could work for weeks at a time. There, these people could make tests and experiments, and do things that can't be done on Earth.

The Soviet Union launched the first space laboratory in 1971. Called *Salyut 1,* it was a big cylinder, forty-seven feet (14 meters) long. It made its own power for heat, light, and air conditioning; contained instruments and machinery; and had sleeping quarters for the people who would live and work on it.

Salyut 1 was launched with no one aboard. But several weeks later, three cosmonauts guided a Soyuz spacecraft to Salyut 1 and docked with it. The men spent twenty-two days aboard Salyut 1. Then, while returning to Earth on the Soyuz, they died in an accident.

After some time, Salyut 1's orbit began to drop nearer to Earth. Finally, the laboratory fell into the atmosphere and burned up. But during the next ten years, the Soviet Union put five more Salyuts into orbit. Crews of cosmonauts and scientists, sent up in Soyuz craft, stayed on each of these. One of the crews that stayed aboard Salyut 6 set a record for time spent in space—96 days, from December 11, 1977, to March 16, 1978.

The U.S. space laboratory Skylab, orbiting Earth.

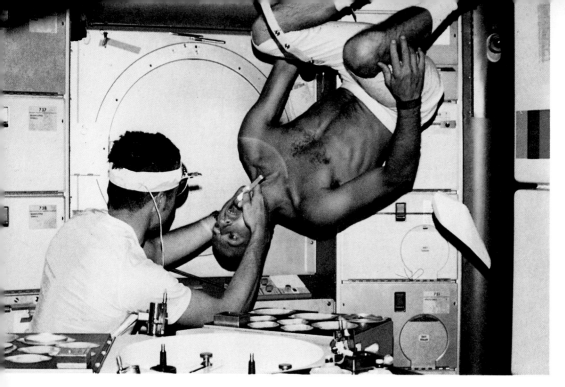

A Skylab astronaut who is also a doctor (above) checks a crewmate's throat. In space, as you can see, there is no "up" or "down." Another Skylab astronaut (below) takes a shower in a special tub.

In 1973, the United States put a space laboratory called Skylab into orbit. However, it was badly damaged during the launching and had to be repaired before it could be used. Three astronauts, sent up in an Apollo spacecraft, put Skylab back to work. Then they became its first crew, working aboard it for twenty-eight days.

During 1973 and 1974, two more crews worked in Skylab. One group spent fifty-nine days aboard the laboratory, the other spent eighty-four days.

Then, the United States had to abandon Skylab because it was beginning to slip closer to Earth's

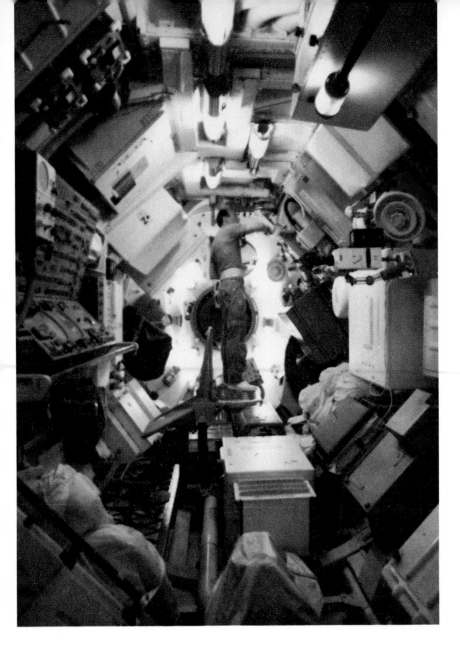

Before going up to Skylab, astronauts had to train in a full-sized model Skylab here on Earth.

atmosphere. In 1979, it fell into the atmosphere and was destroyed.

But the work done in all these space laboratories was important and useful. Scientists learned a great many things. In years to come, permanent laboratories that won't drop back into the atmosphere will be put into orbit.

The space shuttles

Until 1981, every craft that took someone into space and back was either ball-shaped or cone-shaped. These craft, without wings or tail, couldn't possibly fly in Earth's atmosphere. So, once they entered the atmosphere they began to fall at tremendous speed. The only way they could get down safely was by means of huge parachutes.

But that changed in 1981 when the United States sent up the space shuttle *Columbia*. For, while *Columbia* left Earth like a rocket, thundering up into space on spouting flame, it came back like an airplane, gliding down through the atmosphere to make a smooth landing. *Columbia* was the first of a new kind of spacecraft, one with wings and a tail.

At launch, *Columbia* was fastened to a gigantic fuel tank and two big booster rockets needed to lift the heavy, 122-foot (36.6-meter) craft into space. Just before *Columbia* reached the edge of space, the booster rockets ran out of fuel. They were dropped on parachutes, to be recovered and used again.

The space shuttle
Columbia blasting off.

When the giant fuel tank was empty, it was also dropped. No attempt was made to save it, so it burned up as it fell through Earth's atmosphere.

Now that *Columbia* was in space, a quick burst from two small engines put it into orbit. When the pilot was ready to return to Earth, another quick burst sent *Columbia* back into the atmosphere. It was moving so fast that it glowed red with heat. But a covering of heat-resistant tiles on its wings

When the space shuttle's giant fuel tank is empty, it is cast loose. The tank burns up as it falls back through Earth's atmosphere.

A space shuttle flies down through the atmosphere and lands like an airplane.

and body protected it. And because of its wings and tail, it could fly as an airplane. So, it came in for a landing instead of dropping by parachute.

Columbia's first flight, on April 12, 1981, was just a test to see how the craft worked. After that, it began to do the job it had been built for—delivering things into space. *Columbia* has a large cargo hold and can carry satellites into space and put them into orbit. This is much cheaper and easier than launching satellites by rocket.

In November 1983, *Columbia* carried in its cargo hold a "space laboratory" 23 feet (6.9 m) long. Several scientists rode along, to spend nine days making tests and experiments in the laboratory.

Challenger, the second space shuttle, went into space in August 1983. Its job was to put a weather satellite into orbit and make some tests. A year later, after two failures, *Discovery* was launched. It put three communications satellites into orbit. Present plans call for one more space shuttle to be built.

Columbia, *Challenger*, and *Discovery* are called "shuttles" because the word *shuttle* means something that moves back and forth between two places. And this is exactly what these spaceships are intended to do. Before long, they will be making regularly scheduled trips into space.

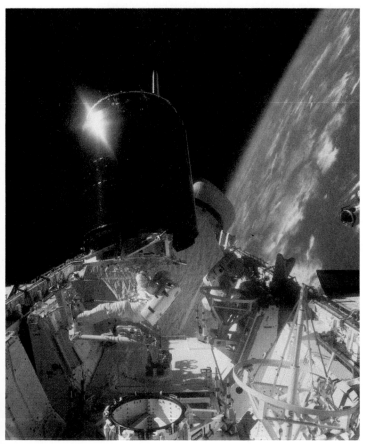

An astronaut (above) stands on the space shuttle *Discovery*'s mechanical arm to take a satellite out of orbit for repair. The satellite (left) is then brought into *Discovery*'s cargo bay. A television picture (below) shows astronauts Sally Ride and Frederick Hauck inside the shuttle *Challenger*.

A jet-propelled American astronaut flies toward a satellite in space.

Human spaceships

During the first twenty-five years of space flight, many men took "spacewalks," floating in space at the ends of long lifelines attached to their spacecraft. But in 1984, two men took a new kind of spacewalk. They left their craft and went out into space about 175 miles (280 kilometers) above the earth, without lifelines.

The men were American astronauts Bruce McCandless and Robert L. Stewart. They and three other astronauts rode the space shuttle *Challenger* into orbit on February 4, 1984. Four days later, McCandless went outside *Challenger* and floated off into space.

Strapped to his back was a machine that looked like a white aluminum armchair without a seat. It was a jet-propelled backpack that enabled him to move about like a miniature spaceship.

Controls on the arms operated the backpack's two sets of jets. Carefully working the jets, McCandless moved out slowly some 150 feet (45 meters) from *Challenger*. Moving backward, he kept his face toward the shuttle so that he wouldn't lose sight of it.

At this moment, McCandless was himself in orbit—a human satellite moving around Earth at a speed of four miles (6.4 km) per second. But to McCandless, it seemed as if he were slowly drifting. He jetted on out to 320 feet (96 m) from the shuttle and practiced turning and moving up and down. "This is neat!" he told the other astronauts through the radio in his space suit's helmet. After ninety minutes, he returned to the shuttle. Later, Stewart went out to test the backpack.

These tests were tremendously important. There is no way to do some of the things that will have to be done in space unless people can move about freely.

Nine months later, in November 1984, the tests proved their real value. Spacewalkers from *Discovery* brought back to the cargo hold two satellites that had failed to go into their proper orbits.

With a jet-propelled backpack, an astronaut is a human spacecraft.

Dropping in on Jupiter

Jupiter, the solar system's largest planet, is a gigantic ball of liquid hydrogen surrounded by thick, swirling clouds. Winds stronger than the strongest hurricanes on Earth roar through those clouds, accompanied by titanic lightning bolts that could "fry" an entire city on Earth. Some time in 1988, a visitor from Earth will drift down through those forbidding storm-swept clouds on a giant parachute in search of information.

The visitor will be an explorer craft, launched from a larger craft, *Galileo*. The *Galileo*, named for one of the greatest scientists, is due to be launched in 1986 and will arrive at Jupiter about two years later.

Galileo and the little explorer craft will be packed with instruments designed to gather information about Jupiter and its moons. As *Galileo* moves toward Jupiter, it will pass

near four of the main moons and will take
many close-up pictures and form them into
maps. It will also take special infrared
pictures that will show what the moons are
formed of.

Then *Galileo* will go into orbit around
Jupiter. The little explorer will be sent down
into the huge planet's atmosphere. As it
drifts down on its huge parachute, it will
check the temperature in the clouds and
make tests to find out exactly what chemicals
the atmosphere contains. It will test for
radiation and measure the amounts of
lightning. Meanwhile, *Galileo*, circling
overhead, will also make many tests.

Fifty years ago, we knew almost nothing
about Jupiter. By the end of this century,
scientists hope to know almost as much about
Jupiter as we do about Earth.

Working in space

Someday, you may have a job in space. You may spend months at a time in a space station, living and working hundreds of miles (kilometers) above Earth.

By 1995, there will probably be at least two space stations in orbit around Earth. One will belong to the United States and the other to the Soviet Union. There may be others.

These space stations may look strange. They will probably be formed of several huge, tanklike cylinders and giant flat sheets of metal and plastic, all joined together and sticking out in all directions.

The cylinders will be "buildings" in which people will live and work and in which things will be stored. Some of the flat sheets will be solar panels to collect sunlight and turn it into electricity needed for light and heat. Others will be radiator panels, collecting heat as it builds up inside the cylinders and

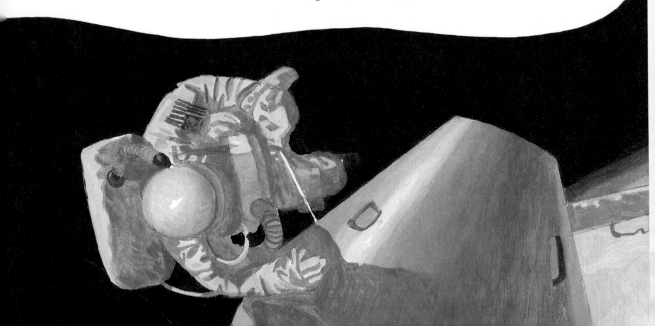

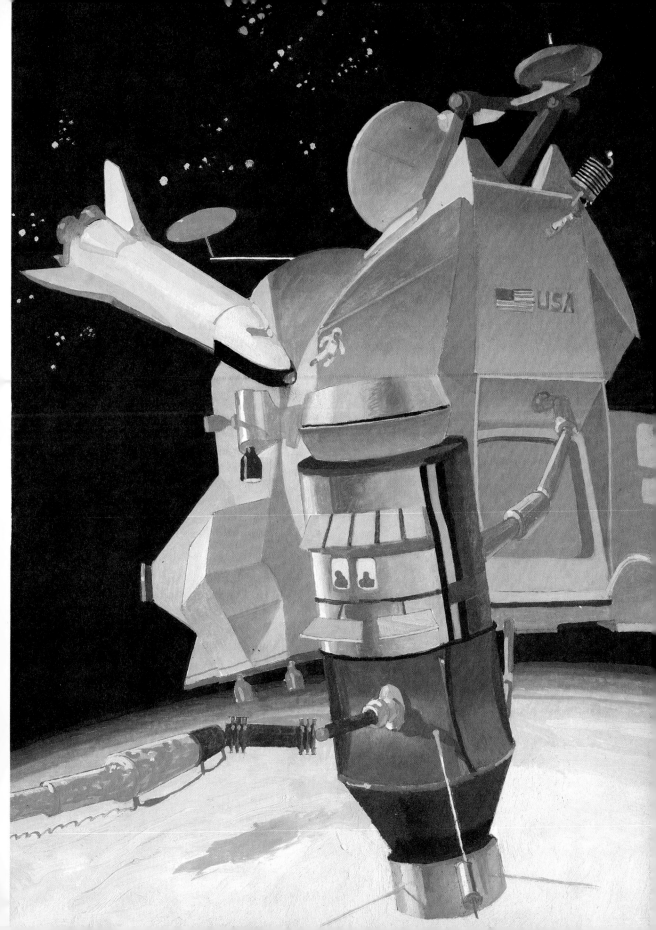

letting it seep out into space. This will keep
the living areas from getting too hot.

The space stations will be built in space.
Walls, panels, machinery, and other things
will be brought into orbit by space shuttles.
Men wearing space suits and jet-propelled
backpacks will then put everything
together—a gigantic construction project
floating in the blackness of space high above
the big blue and white ball of Earth.

Living in a space station will probably be
much like living in a submarine. There won't
be much room, so it will be rather cramped.
People won't have to wear space suits inside
the station, because machines will keep the
cylinder "buildings" heated, lighted, and
air-conditioned. But some space station
workers will probably have to go out into
space regularly. Their "working clothes" will
be space suits and jet-propelled backpacks.

Space stations will do experiments and
scientific work. Some parts of a space station
might become regular factories, producing
things that will be used on Earth. These
space stations will be permanent—that is,
they will stay in place. This will make it
easier to do things that might take a very
long time.

Space station workers will probably spend
as much as six months at a time out in space,
working at their jobs. For a vacation, they
will come back down to Earth.

Meanwhile, Back on Earth...

Modern balloonists

We have sent spacecraft to explore planets billions of miles (kilometers) from Earth. We have space shuttles that go into space and back with ease. We have jet planes that can fly faster than sound.

But some people still like good old-fashioned balloons. People who own balloons and love to go ballooning have formed clubs in many parts of the world.

These people would rather go up in a balloon than fly in an airplane. The clubs hold balloon rallies, balloon races, and other ballooning contests.

Anyone can go up in a balloon, but not just anyone can fly one. In the United States, you must have a pilot's license to fly a balloon. To get a license, you must go to "school" to learn all about ballooning and pass two tests. And the license costs more than a thousand dollars. For that matter, balloons cost a lot—more than ten thousand dollars.

The balloons of today are, of course, much improved over the balloons of long ago. Balloons used to be made of oiled silk, which was rather flimsy. Today they are made of nylon cloth or cotton coated with rubber, and are tough and sturdy.

Most European balloonists still prefer to fill their balloons with hydrogen gas, as most balloonists did during the 1800's. But Americans and Canadians have gone back to the earliest means of getting a balloon into the sky—hot air. The first balloons were hot-air balloons, but people stopped using hot air because of the danger of fire. Today, it is safe. Instead of open fires in fire pans, balloonists now use gas burners that can switch on and off in an instant and shoot out a blast of fire that quickly heats the air.

Balloons may be an old-fashioned idea, but they're a lot of fun to fly.

The crew of *Double Eagle II* had to throw everything out of the gondola to keep their balloon from falling into the ocean.

Ballooning across the oceans

A cheering crowd watched a huge silver and black balloon come drifting down near the little town of Miserey, France, on August 17, 1978. The balloon was finishing a journey of 3,233 miles (5,203 kilometers) that began in the United States. It was the first balloon to cross the Atlantic Ocean.

During the 195 years from 1783, when the first balloon went up, to 1978, seventeen people had tried to fly a balloon across the ocean. None of them had made it, and five died trying. Now, finally, it had been done. Three Americans—Ben Abruzzo, Maxie Anderson, and Larry Newman—rode in the gondola of the balloon, *Double Eagle II*. They took off from Maine on August 11. Westerly winds carried them out over the ocean.

Almost at once, things began to go wrong. First, most of the radio equipment stopped working. Then, about halfway across the ocean, the top of the balloon became coated with ice. This extra weight began to drag the balloon down toward the water. The three men started throwing things out of the gondola, to lighten it. Finally, after the balloon had dropped twenty-five hundred feet (750 meters), the descent was stopped.

But as the balloon neared Ireland, it began to drop again. Soon, it was less than four thousand feet (1,200 m) above the water. The men had already thrown out nearly all they could, so they began ripping floorboards out and throwing them overboard. Soon, the balloon started to rise.

Then the wind died. It looked as if *Double Eagle II* wasn't going to make it. But the wind picked up just enough to get the balloon to Miserey. The trip had taken about 137 hours—almost six days.

Three years later, Abruzzo and Newman, together with Rocky Aoki and Ron Clark, flew a balloon across the Pacific Ocean. They took off from Japan on November 10, 1981, and came down in California 84 hours and 31 minutes later—another "first" for the record books.

Double Eagle II, the first balloon to fly across the Atlantic Ocean, makes a landing in France.

Airships today

Probably most of the people in North America and Europe have seen a Goodyear blimp, either "in person" or on television. There are three of these blimps in the United States and one in Europe. They are the only airships in the world that fly regularly, but they are used only for advertising.

The American blimps—*America, Columbia,* and *Mayflower*—are based in Miami, Houston, and Los Angeles. The European blimp, *Europa,* is based in Rome. They were all built by the Goodyear Tire and Rubber

Company. Each blimp is about 160 feet (48 meters) long, and the gondola, or cabin, fastened to the bottom of the huge gas-filled body can hold the pilot and six passengers. Each blimp is powered by two engines with propellers, and generally flies at a speed of 30-40 miles (48-64 kilometers) per hour.

There may soon be other blimps in the sky. Airship Industries, Limited, of Great Britain and Canada, has built two, *Skyship 500* and *Skyship 600*. It hopes that the airships may soon be used in Great Britain, France, and the United States to carry cargo, patrol coasts, and do air and sea rescue work.

Airships of the future

Strange as it may seem in a world of
spacecraft and jet airplanes, old-fashioned
airships—slow-moving, lighter-than-air
vessels—may be much more common in the
future. However, these airships of the future
will not be old-fashioned in how they look or
what they can do.

One kind of airship of the future may be a
huge, round, helium-filled ball with a curved
gondola hanging beneath it. The ball will
spin as it moves through the air, but the
gondola will hang motionless. By spinning,
the ball will have greater "lift," so that it
will rise more easily.

Another kind of airship, called a "heli-stat," will be a combination of a huge blimp and four helicopters. This airship will be as high as a ten-story building and wider than an aircraft carrier.

These new kinds of airships are being built mainly to lift and carry heavy loads, such as timber, pipes for pipelines, girders, and other construction materials. Before you are much older, there may be several different kinds of airships doing this sort of work.

Hang gliders

Less than a hundred years ago, Otto Lilienthal and others sailed through the air by hanging from big gliding wings, trying to learn how to fly. Today, many people do the same thing with hang gliders—just for fun.

A hang glider is simply a big wing attached to an aluminum frame. These gliders fly much better and more easily than did the gliders of long ago. The first hang glider was invented by a scientist who made a wing-shaped parachute he hoped would help spacecraft land more gently. It did not work for spaceships, but people discovered it was a marvelous glider. Soon, a factory was making hang gliders for sale.

The pilot of a hang glider steers by shifting his weight on the control bar.

You take off in a hang glider the same way that Lilienthal and the Wright brothers did—by running down a hillside until the wind lifts the wing. It's possible to make a hang glider sail thousands of feet (meters) into the sky and travel a hundred miles (160 kilometers) or more. In the air, you hang from a harness and steer the glider with a control bar.

However, anyone who wants to fly a hang glider must take lessons and tests. Hang gliding is wonderful fun, but it can be dangerous.

Sailing in the sky

A sailplane is a kind of superglider. It is an airplane without an engine, designed to soar and glide like a bird. Made of very light, smooth materials, it has long, narrow wings that help keep it up. A skillful pilot can keep a sailplane in the air for many hours, travel hundreds of miles (kilometers), and reach a height of eight miles (12.8 km) or more.

Unlike a hang glider, a sailplane has a cockpit in which the pilot sits. There are instruments in the cockpit—a compass, a dial that shows how fast the glider is moving, and another that shows whether it is rising or dropping. There are also controls with which

the pilot can raise or lower movable flaps on the wings and tail. But, like a hang glider, there is nothing to make a sailplane "go" except the pilot's skill.

To get into the air, a sailplane has to be towed by an airplane at the end of a long rope. When the sailplane is between two thousand and three thousand feet (600 to 900 meters) high, the pilot disconnects the tow rope. Then, he or she begins to ride currents of warm air rising from the ground.

Of course, if something goes wrong there is nothing to keep a sailplane from falling—no engine to keep it flying. So, a sailplane pilot usually wears a parachute, just in case. However, sailplaning is really fairly safe.

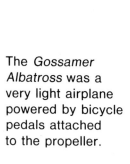

The *Gossamer Albatross* was a very light airplane powered by bicycle pedals attached to the propeller.

Pedaling through the sky

Back in the 1890's, when people were still trying to build a flying machine that would fly, bicycles were common. A few inventors attached bicycle pedals to propellers to get their flying machines to fly. But these "pedal-propelled" airplanes didn't work—the inventors just didn't know enough about machinery or flying.

But in 1979, seventy-six years after the Wright brothers made the first airplane flight, a group of Americans built a pedal-propelled airplane that did work. And on June 12, 1979, a man pedaled it some

twenty-two miles (35.2 kilometers) through the air, across the English Channel.

This airplane was named the *Gossamer Albatross*. (Gossamer is spider silk that floats in air, and an albatross is a large bird with very long wings.) The *Gossamer Albatross* weighed only about seventy-five pounds (33.75 kilograms)—about half of what the man who pedaled it weighed. It had a huge pair of wings, a big propeller, and a tiny, narrow "cabin" for the pilot, all made of lightweight plastic and aluminum.

But light as it was, it wasn't easy to pedal the *Gossamer Albatross* that far. The pilot, Bryan Allen, had to pedal steadily for nearly three hours. All this hard work caused him to perspire heavily. His body lost a great deal of water. When he was only half a mile from the French coast, Allen was so thirsty and in such pain from leg cramps he thought he would have to give up. But he made it.

Why would anyone want to build a plane that has to be pedaled like a bicycle? What good is it?

Well, the people who built *Gossamer Albatross* did want to win the prize money that was offered for the flight. But they also liked the challenge—they wanted to see if they could make it work. And the flight of *Gossamer Albatross* may help us make lighter, faster airplanes in the future.

The pilot of the *Gossamer Albatross* had to pedal steadily for nearly three hours to fly across the English Channel.

Build your own airplane

Have you ever bought a model airplane kit and built a model airplane? Well, how would you like to get a kit with which to build a *real* airplane—one in which you could fly?

Back in the days just after the airplane had been invented, a lot of people built their own airplanes. Those early airplanes were made of such things as varnished silk and bamboo strips to keep them light. They had small, light engines.

But as time went on, airplanes got bigger, heavier, and more complicated. Soon, they were all being built in big factories. People no longer thought about building their own airplanes.

However, new materials and new ideas have appeared. And today, once again, it is possible to build your own plane. A number of companies sell kits containing the parts

and instructions for putting together a small airplane that costs less than an automobile.

These little airplanes are called "ultralights" (meaning "very light") because some of them weigh little more than does an average adult. They are made of very light, tough cloth, and thin, hollow aluminum rods. Like the homemade airplanes of long ago, they have small, lightweight engines.

A kit for an ultralight airplane has everything you need—even the parts for the engine. It takes about forty hours to put the

An ultralight airplane flies past Mont-Saint-Michel in France.

plane together, using ordinary tools. The people who sell the kits must check each plane after it is built, to make sure it's safe. Then they teach the owner how to fly it.

These little airplanes can go as high as four miles (6.4 kilometers) and can fly more than 60 miles (96 km) per hour. They carry enough fuel to stay in the air for about two hours.

Some people think ultralight airplanes are very dangerous. These planes are not permitted to fly in some places.

The "all-around" aircraft

A helicopter is a wingless aircraft. Small helicopters have a large propeller on top that lifts them up and carries them through the air, and a small propeller on the tail that keeps the helicopter from spinning around.

A helicopter can do many things a winged airplane can't do. It can go straight up or down, fly backwards, sideways, or forward, and it can hover, or stay in one place. These things make a helicopter an "all-around" aircraft that is useful in many ways.

Politicians, businessmen, and others who must travel a lot often go by helicopter. They don't have to follow roads, can avoid traffic jams, and can land anywhere—even on the roof of the building where they are going to do business or give a speech. For the same reason, television reporters and camera crews often use helicopters to get quickly to the scene of an important news event.

Because a helicopter can hover and fly in any direction, it is valuable in search and rescue work. It can fly low and slowly over wild, woody places to search for a lost child, or pick up a person trapped on the roof of a house that is surrounded by floodwaters.

Helicopters can also carry heavy loads that are too big or odd-shaped for a truck or an airplane. For example, a helicopter can fly with an eighty-foot (24-meter) radio tower dangling beneath it. And it can set the tower down exactly where it's wanted.

Helicopters can move large numbers of soldiers quickly to where they are needed. Helicopter gunships, armed with special weapons, can hover over one spot and rake enemy troops with gunfire. Military helicopters can also bring ammunition, supplies, artillery, and other heavy equipment into places where no other kind of vehicle could go.

Truly, the "whirlybird" is an all-around aircraft.

The fastest jetliners

By the 1960's, the United States, Russia, and other countries had warplanes that could fly faster than the speed of sound, which is about 740 miles (1,190 kilometers) per hour. But no passenger planes could go that fast.

However, several countries began building supersonic (faster than sound) jet passenger liners in the 1960's. Russia built and tested the first supersonic jetliner, the Tupolev Tu-144, in 1968. The Concorde, built by Great Britain and France, made its first test flight in 1969. Since 1976, the Concorde has made regular passenger flights. These planes can fly at speeds of as much as 1,550 miles (2,494

A Concorde supersonic jetliner can fly from Paris to New York in less than four hours.

km) per hour, and can fly from Paris to New York City in less than four hours.

Many people believed that supersonic transports (SST's) would soon be the only planes carrying passengers across oceans or on other long flights.

But the SST's had problems. They are very noisy, and they use enormous amounts of fuel. Because of this, they are very expensive to run. It costs a lot to ride in them, and few people can afford to pay the price.

And so, the supersonic jetliners never became as important as many people thought they would be. Only sixteen were built. And by the early 1980's, only a few were still in service.

A trip on a jet airplane

You and your parents are sitting in a section of the airport near a sign that says GATE 7. Many other people are seated or standing all around you.

Through huge windows you can look out onto part of the airfield. You see big, silvery jets come sailing down out of the sky to land on a distant part of the field. And you watch as planes climb toward the clouds on their way to distant cities.

Soon, you'll be soaring up into the sky on one of those planes! You and your parents are going to fly to Europe! But you wonder if it's ever going to happen. You have been

sitting here for an hour or more, and it
seems even longer.

Then, suddenly, a voice on a loudspeaker
says, "Flight number 005 to Frankfurt,
Germany, now boarding at Gate Seven."

All around you, there's a stir and bustle as
people begin picking up coats, suitcases, and
packages. A door next to one of the big
windows opens and people start to move
through it. You and your parents pick up
your bags and get into the line heading for
the door.

Passing through the door, you find yourself
in a kind of tunnel that leads into a big jet
airplane. As you step into the plane, a
smiling flight attendant greets you, looks at

your boarding pass, and points in the
direction you must go to find your seat. You
and your parents make your way down the
aisle until you find the seats that match the
numbers on your tickets. What luck—you get
to sit by a window!

You and your parents stow your parcels
beneath the seats and in an overhead
compartment. Excitedly, you wiggle down
into your seat. It has an arm with buttons
and switches on it. You experiment, and find
that one switch turns on a little light above
your head.

The others, your mother explains, are for
changing stations to listen to music on the
radio. There is a set of earphones in a plastic

bag in a pouch on the back of the seat in front of you. Your mother shows you how to connect them to an opening in the seat arm and fit them into your ears, so you can hear music without disturbing anyone else.

The plane quickly fills with people. You think it will take off as soon as everyone is seated, but it doesn't. There's still some more waiting to do, it seems!

Then, after a time, a soft chime sounds. A sign in front of all the seats lights up with glowing letters that say Please Fasten Your Seat Belt. The flight attendants hurry up and down the aisles to help anyone who can't get his or her seat belt properly fastened.

A voice on the loudspeaker calmly explains what to do in case there should be an emergency. Flight attendants, standing at the front of each aisle, demonstrate how to put on an oxygen mask. In an emergency, an oxygen mask will drop down to you from a compartment overhead. You would need that mask if something went wrong, because the plane flies so high there's no air to breathe outside the cabin. However, such emergencies almost never occur. The attendants also show the passengers how to use the life jackets, because the plane will be flying over the ocean, and where the emergency doors are located.

Now you become aware of the humming engines as the huge jet begins to move. It

taxis slowly out onto a runway. Now it pauses for a moment. Then, suddenly, the sound of the engines becomes a loud roar. You begin to roll forward, faster and faster and faster. The ground seems to be whizzing by. And then you're aware of a different feeling. The plane isn't rolling along the ground anymore—it is in the air!

As you look out the window, the ground appears to fall away from under you. You can see the highway that runs near the

airport. It seems no wider than a ribbon, and the cars on it are no bigger than bugs.

The plane climbs steeply, and after a moment you see only bright sky. Moments later, a white haze seems to cover your window. The plane is going through clouds.

The plane continues to climb. Then you feel it level off. It has reached its proper height and is on the right path for the long flight to come. Now, when you look out the window you see bright blue sky all around you. And far below is a vast sea of white clouds. The clouds look like millions of gobs of whipped cream stuck together.

Now you can unfasten your seat belt and relax. You can listen to music, talk to your parents, or read the book you brought along. There's nothing to see out the window except the sea of whipped-cream clouds.

Time passes. Just when you realize you're getting hungry, flight attendants begin pushing large carts down the aisles. The carts are crowded with silvery packages. It is dinnertime.

Your mother shows you how to pull down the little table that's on the back of the seat in front of you. The flight attendant hands you a tray with one of the silvery packages, and a plastic knife, fork, and spoon, wrapped in a paper napkin. You strip off the silver foil—careful, it's hot—and find a tray with compartments filled with good, warm things

to eat. These dinners were cooked before
they were put on board. Then they were kept
in a refrigerator on the plane, and heated up
in a special microwave oven.

After dinner, there is a movie to watch.
The screen is in front of the rows of seats,
and you listen to the sound through
earphones.

When the movie is over you look out the window. It's dark outside now. You can't see anything but stars overhead. However, there probably wouldn't be much to see anyway. The pilot, talking over the loudspeaker, has announced that the plane is over the Atlantic Ocean.

Before long you feel sleepy. One of the buttons on your seat makes it tilt back. You lean back, close your eyes, and soon you are asleep.

You awaken to a great deal of bustle. The plane is still dark, but the sky is light outside your window. It's morning, and the flight

attendants hurry to awaken everyone and
bring them rolls, jam, juice, and coffee. The
pilot announces over the loudspeaker that the
plane will be landing in Frankfurt, Germany,
in about an hour. By the time you have
finished your breakfast, you can see
grayish-green countryside far below. Europe!

The plane gradually drops lower. The soft
chime rings again—time to fasten your seat
belt for the landing. Through the window,
you can now make out roads no wider than
pieces of string, with tiny specks moving on
them. Sunlight flashes on a winding silver
ribbon that must be a river.

Before long you can make out treetops and
the roofs of buildings. As you watch,
everything seems to grow bigger and move
closer. In moments, you are looking down at
the broad, gray airport runway. Now, the
plane is level with nearby rooftops and
treetops.

Suddenly, you feel a slight bump and hear a sharp squeak. The plane's wheels have touched the ground and it is rolling swiftly along the runway. It slows as it approaches the terminal, and then comes to a stop.

It hardly seems possible that only eight hours ago you were in the United States, and now you're in Germany. Less than sixty years ago, it took Charles Lindbergh more than four times as long to fly from New York to Paris. And seventy-five years ago, no airplane could even fly such a distance.

But you are living in the Age of Flight. Sky and space have been conquered!

Books to Read

There are many good books about airplanes and aviation, and about space vehicles and space travel. A few are listed here. Your school library or public library will have some of these, as well as many others.

Ages 5 to 8

The Astronauts by Dinah L. Moche (Random House, 1978)
Here is a simple account of how astronauts train for a space flight, and the things they must do while in space.

The Challenge of Space by Robin Kerrod (Lerner, 1980)
Such topics as: What kinds of people become astronauts? and how people live in satellites are covered in question-and-answer form in this book.

Dangerous Adventure! Lindbergh's Famous Flight by Ruth Belov Gross (Walker, 1977)
This book gives a very clear picture of the dangers and risks that this young pilot took in the early days of aviation.

Finding Out About Rockets and Spaceflight by Lynn Myring (Educational Development Corporation, 1982)
Clearly presented information and colorful illustrations and diagrams answer young children's questions, such as: "Where do astronauts sleep?" and "What do astronauts eat?" The book also clearly explains possible and impossible future situations in space flight.

The First Book of Airplanes by Jeanne Bendick (Watts, 1976)
With text and pictures aimed especially at younger readers, this book explains how airplanes fly, describes some of the early days of aviation, and even covers the operation of an airplane.

The Glorious Flight: Across the Channel with Louis Blériot by Alice and Martin Provensen (Viking, 1983)
A beautifully illustrated book that describes the many problems and disappointments suffered by the French aviator Louis Blériot, before he finally became the first person to fly across the English Channel in an airplane.

Let's Go to the Moon by Janis Knudsen Wheat (National Geographic Society, 1977)
Exciting photographs, illustrations, and text work together to tell the story of the *Apollo 17* flight to the moon and back.

Satellites by Alice Fields (Watts, 1981)
The many photographs and diagrams in this book help to simplify explanations of the artificial satellites that have been launched from Earth.

Space by Susan Harris (Watts, 1979)
This is an introduction to the makeup of the solar system, the functions of rockets and satellites, and the problems that humans face in space.

Spacecraft by Jay Miceal (Watts, 1983)
An "Easy-Read Fact Book" for young readers, *Spacecraft* pictures and describes many of the satellites now orbiting earth, covers current space vehicles, and stirs the imagination with glimpses of such future possibilities as vacations in space.

Take Me Out to the Airfield! How the Wright Brothers Invented the Airplane by Robert Quackenbush (Parents, 1976)
In this book, a pilot in an airport tells two young children the story of the Wright brothers. The book includes a simple explanation of how an airplane flies, and provides a plan for making a model glider.

True Book of the Mars Landing by Leila Boyle Gemme (Childrens Press, 1977)
This is the story of the exploration of the planet Mars, with special attention paid to the work of the two Viking spacecraft landers that tested the Martian soil for life.

The True Book of Spinoffs from Space by Leila Boyle Gemme (Childrens Press, 1977)
This book shows how ideas and machinery developed for space flight have helped improve ways of doing many things on earth. Medical care, weather forecasting, food processing, protection of the environment, and clothing design have all benefited from the exploration of space.

Ages 9 to 12

Aircraft That Work for Us by Tony Freeman (Childrens Press, 1981)
The use of aircraft for news reporting, pest control, emergency services, and to meet many other needs is covered in text and action-packed photographs.

Album of Spaceflight by Tom McGowen (Rand, 1983)
Here is a brief history of humanity's conquest of space, from the launching of Sputnik to the space shuttles.

Balloon Trip: A Sketchbook by Huck Scarry (Prentice-Hall, 1983)
This is a book that tells what it is like to fly in a balloon. It also provides interesting information on how a balloon is made, and on the history of ballooning. The book contains many sketches the author made while flying in balloons.

Blimps by Tony Freeman (Childrens Press, 1979)
This is an outstanding book about the kind of airship known as a "blimp."

Colonizing Space by Erik Bergaust (Putnam, 1978)
This book tells how space colonies can be established in the solar system and what life on them may be like.

Early Birds: An Informal Account of the Beginnings of Aviation by John Halpern (Dutton, 1980)
Here is the story of the fun, adventure, uncertainty, and danger of aviation in the years between World Wars I and II.

Helicopters by Susan Harris (Watts, 1979)
In this history of helicopters, readers will learn how these whirlybirds fly, and the many ways in which they are used today.

How Did We Find Out About Outer Space? by Isaac Asimov (Walker, 1977)
This is the story of all the inventions and discoveries, from earliest times to the present, that led up to our space-going abilities of today.

Man in Space to the Moon by Franklyn M. Branley (Crowell, 1970)
This book offers the complete story of the voyage that landed the first man on the moon—how the astronauts lived

and worked in space, how they made the landing, their exploration of the moon, and their return to earth.

Neil Armstrong, Space Pioneer by Paul Westman (Lerner, 1980)
This is a biography of the first person to set foot on the moon.

New York to Nome: The First International Cross-Country Flight by Marian Place (Macmillan, 1972)
In 1920, four small airplanes made of wood, wire, and cloth set out on the first cross-country flight, from New York City to Nome, Alaska. This is the story of that dangerous, exciting, three-month long adventure.

Out to Launch: Model Rockets by Ross Olney (Lothrop, 1979)
This book offers a treasury of information for both advanced and beginning model rocket enthusiasts.

The Paper Airplane Book by Seymour Simon (Viking, 1971)
Here is information on how to make paper airplanes with rudders, elevators, and flaps—showing graphically the basic facts of flight.

Satellites by Alice Fields (Watts, 1981)
This book contains information about the kinds of satellites that have been sent into space—satellites for weather study, astronomy, communications, etc.

See Inside a Space Station by Robin Kerrod (Watts, 1978)
The author provides information about how the space stations, planned by both the U.S. and Soviet Union, will be built and manned.

Skystars: The History of Women in Aviation by Ann Hodgman and Rudy Djabbaroff (Atheneum, 1981)
Both girls and boys will be interested in these true accounts of women who were involved in the early days of ballooning, airships, airplanes, stunt flying, aerial warfare, and space exploration.

Space Flight by Stewart Cowley (Warwick, 1982)
This account covers the Space Age from the early rocket experiments to the first flight of the space shuttle.

Space Science by Christopher Lampton (Franklin Watts, 1983)
This dictionary-style book clearly explains the meanings of terms dealing with space flight and astronomy.

What Makes a Plane Fly? by Scott Corbett (Atlantic-Little, Brown, 1967)
This book combines easy-to-follow text and helpful diagrams to explain the principles of flight.

Windows in Space by Ann Elwood and Linda C. Wood (Walker, 1982)
This book, for thoughtful young readers, provides information on the solar system and beyond, on human problems of space flight, and on the possibilities of space flight beyond the solar system and life on other worlds in the far reaches of space.

Yesterday's Airplanes by Don Berliner (Lerner, 1980)
In this book, you will find good photographs and brief descriptions of pioneer planes of the first fifty years of flight—from the Wright brothers' *Flyer* of 1903 to the 1947 Monocouple.

New Words

Here are some of the words you have met in this book. Many of them may be new to you. All are useful words to know. Next to each word, you'll see how to say the word: **aerial** (AIR ee uhl). The part in capital letters is said more loudly than the rest of the word. One or two sentences tell what the word means.

aerial (AIR ee uhl)
Aerial means anything having to do with flying or aircraft.

airship (AIR shihp)
An airship is a lighter-than-air aircraft. It is a balloon, filled with gas, that has its own motive power and can be steered in any direction. It is also called a dirigible or a blimp. *See also* **zeppelin.**

altitude (AL tuh tood)
Altitude is height above the ground.

antenna (an TEHN uh)
An antenna is a long metal rod or wire used for sending or receiving radio signals.

antiaircraft gun (an ty AIR kraft guhn)
An antiaircraft gun is a kind of cannon that can fire an exploding shell high into the air to damage or destroy enemy aircraft.

atmosphere (AT muh sfihr)
Atmosphere is the layer of gas or gases that surrounds the surface of some planets and moons. Earth's atmosphere is called air.

biplane (BY playn)
A biplane is an airplane that has two wings, one above the other.

booster (BOOS tuhr)
A booster is a device for increasing the power or thrust of an engine. A booster rocket helps push a spacecraft into space.

Celsius (SEHL see uhs)
Celsius is the name of the scale used for centigrade (metric) thermometers. Water freezes at 0 degrees Celsius and boils at 100 degrees Celsius. *See also* **Fahrenheit.**

cylinder (SIHL uhn duhr)
A cylinder is a tube with flat ends. A tin can is a cylinder.

diagonal (dy AG uh nuhl)
A diagonal is a straight, slanted line. Military aircraft sometimes fly in a diagonal formation, with the lowest plane ahead of the highest one.

dirigible (DIHR uh juh buhl or duh RIHJ uh buhl), *see* **airship.**

Fahrenheit (FAR uhn hyt)
Fahrenheit is the name of the scale used for measuring temperature in the United States and some other places. Water freezes at 32 degrees Fahrenheit and boils at 212 degrees Fahrenheit. *See also* **Celsius.**

float (floht)
A float is a hollow, cigar-shaped device. On a seaplane, two floats take the place of wheels and keep the plane afloat in water.

friction (FRIHK shuhn)
Friction is the rubbing of one thing against another, causing heat. The longer and faster this rubbing takes place, the hotter both things get. It is friction that causes an object falling from space into Earth's atmosphere to burn up.

goggles (GAHG uhlz)
Goggles are large, tight-fitting eyeglasses worn by aviators flying open-cockpit airplanes to protect their eyes from wind and dust.

gondola (GAHN duh luh)
A gondola is the car or container that hangs beneath a balloon or airship and holds the passengers, controls, instruments, and motors.

helium (HEE lee uhm)
Helium is a gas that is lighter than air and will not burn. It is used in

balloons and airships to make them rise in the air.

hover (HUHV uhr or HAHV uhr)
Hover means to hang in the air without moving, or moving only a little. A helicopter can hover.

hydrogen (HY druh juhn)
Hydrogen is a gas that is lighter than air. It was once used in balloons and airships, but is very dangerous because it burns easily.

Lunar Excursion Module (LOO nuhr ehk skur zhuhn MAHJ ool)
Lunar means "of the moon." An excursion is a trip. A module is a self-contained unit that is part of something else. Thus, the Lunar Excursion Module was a separate part of the spacecraft that made the trip to the moon.

meteorologist (mee tee uh RAHL uh jihst)
A meteorologist is a scientist who studies atmosphere and weather.

monoplane (MAHN uh playn)
A monoplane is an airplane with one wing.

orbit (AWR biht)
An orbit is the path that a smaller object takes around a larger one, in space. The moon moves in an orbit around Earth, and Earth moves in an orbit around the sun. An object is kept in its orbit by the pull of gravity.

oxygen (AHK suh juhn)
Oxygen is a colorless, ordorless, tasteless gas that makes up about one-fifth of Earth's air. Most plants and animals could not live without oxygen to breathe.

physicist (FIHZ uh sihst)
A physicist is a scientist who studies the forces of nature that cause all things in the universe to work as they do.

probe (prohb)
A probe is a device used to explore a place that a person cannot get to.

propeller (pruh PEHL uhr)
A propeller is a set of spinning blades that pull or push an aircraft through the air.

radar (RAY dahr)
Radar is an instrument that uses radio waves to locate unseen objects and measure their distance, speed, and direction.

radiation (ray dee AY shuhn)
Radiation is the giving off of energy such as heat, light, or electricity. The sun gives off radiation.

rotation (roh TAY shuhn)
Rotation is the spinning of an object around its center. The Earth rotates around its axis, an imaginary line between the North and South poles.

runway (RUHN way)
A runway is a straight, smooth stretch of ground on which aircraft take off and land.

shuttle (SHUHT uhl)
A shuttle is a device that moves back and forth. The space shuttle moves back and forth between Earth and space.

stratosphere (STRAT uh sfihr)
The stratosphere is the part of Earth's atmosphere that extends from about ten miles (16 km) to thirty miles (48 km) above the ground.

streamlined (STREEM lynd)
Streamlined means having a shape like a bullet or torpedo that offers the least resistance to air or water.

supersonic (soo puhy SAHN ihk)
Supersonic means faster than the speed of sound, which is about 740 miles (960 km) per hour.

triplane (TRY playn)
A triplane is an airplane with three wings, one above another.

zeppelin (ZEHP uh luhn or ZEHP luhn)
A zeppelin is any huge, cigar-shaped airship of the type designed by Count Ferdinand von Zeppelin. *See also* **airship.**

Illustration Acknowledgments

The publishers of *Childcraft* gratefully acknowledge the courtesy of the following photographers, agencies, and organizations for illustrations in this volume. When all the illustrations for a sequence of pages are from a single source, the inclusive page numbers are given. Credits should be read from left to right, top to bottom, on their respective pages. All illustrations are the exclusive property of the publishers of *Childcraft* unless names are marked with an asterisk (*).

Cover: Aristocrat and Standard Binding—David Wenzel
Heritage Binding—George Guzzi; Steve Lissau,
Gamma/Liaison*; Beverly Pardee; Roberta Polfus;
Jim Tuten, Black Star*; Roberta Polfus; David
Wenzel; FPG*; Tony Gibbons
Discovery Binding—Beverly Pardee

1–3: Elizabeth Miles
8–9: Culver*
10–11: Mou-sien Tseng; Martin Giese
12–13: Martin Giese
14–15: Mou-sien Tseng; Bibliothèque Nationale, Paris (Art Resource)*; Collection of the IBM Corporation*; Ambrosian Library, Milan, Italy (Art Resource)*; Bibliothèque Nationale, Paris (Art Resource)*
16–17: Historical Picture Service*
18–19: Historical Picture Service*; Martin Giese
20–21: Culver*
22–25: David Wenzel
26–27: Arti Ruiz
28–33: David Wenzel
34–35: Culver*; Hal Frenck
36–37: Brown Bros.*; Historical Picture Service*; Arti Ruiz
38–39: Bettmann Archive*
40–41: Hal Frenck
42–43: Hal Frenck; Arti Ruiz
44–45: Culver*
46–49: Beverly Pardee
50–51: Bettmann Archive*
52–53: Tony Gibbons
54–57: Mou-sien Tseng
58–59: Richard Hook
60–61: Library of Congress*
62–63: Ministère de l'Air, Paris*
64–65: Richard Hook; Scott Polar Research Institute*
66–67: Andréemuséet, Gränna, Sweden*; Richard Hook
68–69: Beverly Pardee
70–71: Beverly Pardee; Brown Bros.*
72–73: Tony Gibbons
74–75: Brown Bros.*
76–77: Mou-sien Tseng
78–79: Archiv Krueger*; Historical Picture Service*
80–81: Martin Giese; Library of Congress*
82–83: Tony Gibbons
84–85: Brian Watson; Smithsonian Institution, National Air Museum*
86–87: Richard Hook; Library of Congress*
88–89: Richard Hook
90–91: Library of Congress*
92–93: Richard Hook; Martin Giese
94–95: Mou-sien Tseng; Bettmann Archive*
96–97: Tony Gibbons; Bettmann Archive*
98–99: Chicago Historical Society*; Library of Congress*; Brian Watson

100–101: Martin Giese
102–103: Mou-sien Tseng
104–105: Library of Congress*; Culver*; Bettmann Archive*
106–107: Brian Watson; Martin Giese
108–109: Bettmann Archive*
110–111: Jim Pearson
112–113: Hal Frenck; Jim Pearson; Granger Collection*
114–115: Louis Vallin Collection*; Bert Dodson; George Guzzi
116–123: George Guzzi
124–125: World Book photos; Hal Frenck; Brown Bros.*; Culver*
126–127: Jim Pearson
128–129: Jim Pearson; Imperial War Museum*; Culver*; Hal Frenck
130–131: Bert Dodson; Musée de la Guerre*
132–133: Bert Dodson; Jim Pearson
134–135: Bettmann Archive*
136–137: Culver*; Brown Bros.*; Chris Calle
138–139: George Guzzi; Culver*
140–141: Chris Calle
142–143: Francis Livingston
144–145: Bettmann Archive*; Francis Livingston; FPG*
146–147: Bettmann Archive*; Chris Calle
148–149: Esther C. Goddard*; Arti Ruiz
150–151: Francis Livingston; Bettmann Archive*
152–153: UPI/Bettmann Archive*
154–155: Arti Ruiz; Brown Bros.*
156–157: Bettmann Archive*; Francis Livingston
158–159: Culver*
160–161: George Guzzi
162–163: Bettmann Archive*
164–165: George Guzzi; Culver*
166–167: George Guzzi
168–169: George Guzzi; Culver*
170–171: Chris Calle
172–173: Imperial War Museum*
174–175: National Archives*; Arti Ruiz
176–177: Arti Ruiz
178–179: Bettmann Archive*
180–181: George Guzzi
182–183: U.S. Air Force*; Bettmann Archive*
184–185: U.S. Air Force*
186–189: George Guzzi
190–191: NASA*
192–193: Sovfoto*
194–195: NASA*
196–197: Roberta Polfus
198–199: Richard Hook; Yoshi Miyake
200–203: Richard Hook
204–209: Jim Pearson
210–215: NASA*
216–217: NASA*; Tony Gibbons
218–219: AP/Wide World*; NASA*
220–221: NASA*; Roberta Polfus
222–225: Terry Hadler
226–227: Yoshi Miyake
228–231: Brian Watson
232–233: Brian Watson; Jet Propulsion Laboratory*
234–237: NASA*
238–239: Yoshi Miyake
240–241: Roberta Polfus
242–243: Tony Gibbons; NASA*
244–245: NASA*
246–247: Jim Tuten, Black Star*; Tony Gibbons; NASA*
248–251: NASA*
252–253: Yoshi Miyake
254–257: Robert Baxter
258–259: David F. Williams, Jr., Picture Group*
260–261: Stephen Kelley, Gamma/Liaison*
262–263: Jennifer Emry-Perrott; Alain Keler, Sygma*
264–265: Shelly Katz, Black Star*
266–267: Hal Frenck
268–269: Jennifer Emry-Perrott; Steve Lissau, Gamma/Liaison*
270–271: Hal Frenck
272–273: Philippe Achache, Gamma/Liaison*
274–275: Alain Nogues, Sygma*; Jennifer Emry-Perrott
276–277: Eric Preau, Sygma*
278–279: Hal Frenck
280–281: Dennis Brack, Black Star*
282–291: Hal Frenck

Index

This index is an alphabetical list of the important topics covered in this book. It will help you find information given in both words *and* pictures. To help you understand what an entry means, there is often a helping word in parentheses. For example, **ace** (aviator). If there is information in both words and pictures, you will see the words *with pictures* after the page number. If there is *only* a picture, you will see the word *picture* before the page number.

Preface

There have probably always been some people who dreamed of flying and of visiting the moon and stars. Some of our oldest stories and legends show this. But for thousands of years, this seemed to be an impossible dream—even though a few people tried to fly by fastening artificial wings to their arms.

Then, about four hundred years ago, in Europe, there was a sudden surge of desire to find out new things and to learn what makes things happen. People began to experiment and try out things no one had dared do before. And in time—little more than two hundred years ago—human beings discovered how to fly by using balloons.

That was the beginning of the conquest of sky and space. The story of what has happened since then is one of the most thrilling, awesome—and often funny—stories in all of human history.

And here it is.

Contents

Conquest of the Sky

A supplement to
Childcraft—The How and Why Library

World Book, Inc.
a Scott Fetzer company

Chicago London Sydney Toronto

Conquest of the Sky